225 SPECIES IN FULL COLOR

INSECTS

A GUIDE TO FAMILIAR AMERICAN INSECTS

by
HERBERT S. ZIM, Ph.D.
and
CLARENCE COTTAM, Ph.D.

Illustrated by
JAMES GORDON IRVING

1991 Scholars Edition
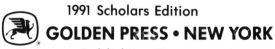
GOLDEN PRESS • NEW YORK
Western Publishing Company, Inc.
Racine, Wisconsin

FOREWORD

This book is one of the most ambitious attempted in the Golden Guide series. Because of its scope, unusual problems had to be solved all along the way. The end was achieved because of the cooperation of many people who felt it important to have a reliable beginner's guide to insects. The authors express their appreciation to all who participated.

The artist, James Gordon Irving, made a superb contribution. His wife, Grace Crowe Irving, helped in field studies, collecting, and research. Robert T. Mitchell was most helpful—in compiling lists from which the original selections were made; in checking data; in preparing maps. Specimens came from the Patuxent Wildlife Research Center, the U.S. National Museum, and Melville W. Osborne, Rahway, N. J. Numerous specialists generously offered suggestions on the plates—William D. Field, Edward A. Chapin, William H. Anderson, Austin H. Clark, George B. Vogt, Reece I. Sailer, Hahn W. Capps, O. L. Cartwright, Paul W. Oman, Ashley B. Gurney, Barnard D. Burks, Karl V. Krombein, Ross H. Arnett, Jr., Marion R. Smith, Alan Stone, John G. Franclemont, Arthur B. Gahan, Curtis W. Sabrosky, Grace B. Glance, C. F. W. Muesebeck, and others. We wish to acknowledge Jean Laffoon's help in checking the text and plates.

We are grateful to Allen M. Young, Ph.D., Curator and Head, Invertebrate Zoology, Milwaukee Public Museum, for preparing the current revision.

H.S.Z. and C.C.

Revised Edition, 1987

By dealing only with common, important, and showy insects, this book will help the novice begin a fascinating study. To identify an insect, turn to the key to the insect groups (orders) on pages 4 and 5. Insects are grouped by orders; each order contains insects with certain characters in common. Compare your specimen with the illustrated example used to represent an order and look for similar features. Carefully read the descriptions of the different groups to find out which fits your specimen best. When you think you know to what order your insect belongs, turn to the pages given. There you will find more insects of that order for comparison with yours. A strong magnifying lens will be very helpful.

Insects in this book are often shown on their food plants. Immature forms often appear with the adult. If you cannot identify an immature insect, try to rear it to maturity.

In advanced study the Latin scientific names of species are used for greater precision in designation. Scientific names of species illustrated in this book are given on pages 155-157.

On plates, approximate lengths are given in inches ("w." indicates wingspread).

Range maps show occurrence of species within the United States, just over the Mexican border, and about 200 miles northward into Canada. Since distribution of many species is little known, ranges given are only approximate. Where ranges of two or more insects appear on one map, each has a different color or line pattern, as in the sample here. A red tint over a line pattern indicates greater abundance (as on page 17). Each caption is on or next to the color to which it refers.

GRASSHOPPERS, ROACHES, AND THEIR KIN (Orthoptera), pages 17-28. Medium to large insects. Live on land. Forewings leathery. Hindwings folded fan-like (some have no wings). Development gradual. Chewing mouth-parts.

EARWIGS (Dermaptera), page 29. Medium insects with typical pincer-like tail. Usually have two pairs of short wings. Segmented antennae. Development gradual.

TERMITES (Isoptera), pages 30-31. Ant-like insects, small and soft-bodied. Some have four long wings. Live in colonies. Specialized "castes" for working, fighting. Chewing mouth-parts. Development gradual.

LICE (Anoplura), page 32. Tiny, wingless insects with piercing and sucking mouth-parts. Body flattened. Legs with claws for clinging to warm-blooded animals.

LEAFHOPPERS, APHIDS, SCALE INSECTS, AND CICADAS (Homoptera), pages 33-41. Small to medium insects, most with two pairs of similar wings held sloping at sides of body. Jointed beak for sucking attached to base of head. Land insects. Some scale-like.

TRUE BUGS (Hemiptera), pages 42-49. Range from small to large in size. Two pairs of wings, with forewings partly thickened. Jointed beak for sucking arises from front of head. Development is gradual.

DRAGONFLIES AND DAMSELFLIES (Odonata), pages 50-51. Medium to large insects with two pairs of long, equal-sized wings. Body long and slender. Antennae short. Immature stages are aquatic. Development in three stages.

MAYFLIES (Ephemerida) **AND STONEFLIES** (Plecoptera), page 52. Both with two pairs of transparent, veined wings. In mayflies, hindwings smaller; in stoneflies, larger. Mayflies have long, pronged tails. Immatures aquatic.

5

NERVE-WINGED INSECTS (Neuroptera), pages 53-55. Large insects. The two pairs of wings, usually equal in size, are netted with veins. Four stages of development: egg, larva, pupa, and adult. Chewing mouth-parts. Long antennae.

SCORPIONFLIES (Mecoptera), page 56. Medium-sized insects with two pairs of slender, generally spotted wings. Legs long. Antennae long also. Beak-like, chewing mouth-parts. Larvae live in soil.

CADDISFLIES (Trichoptera), page 57. Small to medium-sized insects. Most larvae live in fresh water. Some build ornamented case. Adults with two pairs of wings with long, silky hairs and with long antennae. Mouth-parts reduced.

MOTHS AND BUTTERFLIES (Lepidoptera), pages 58-101. Small to large insects with two pairs of scaly wings. Sucking mouth-parts, sometimes reduced. Antennae knob-like or feathery. Development in four stages.

FLIES AND THEIR KIN (Diptera), pages 102-108. Two-winged, tiny to medium insects, with sucking mouth-parts. Antennae small, eyes large. Second pair of wings reduced to balancing organs. Development in four stages.

BEETLES (Coleoptera), pages 109-135. Forewings modified to thickened covers. Hindwings thin, folded. Size from tiny to large. Chewing mouth-parts. Antennae usually short. All have four life stages. Some aquatic.

BEES, WASPS, AND ANTS (Hymenoptera), pages 136-149. Tiny to large insects; many social or colonial. Two pairs of thin, transparent wings. Hindwings smaller. Mouth-parts for chewing or sucking. Only insects with "stingers." Development in four stages.

SEEING INSECTS

Insects are found everywhere, even in the Antarctic. They have been on this earth some 200 million years, and seem here to stay. More insects and more kinds of insects are known than all other animals visible to the naked eye. Insects have been called man's worst enemy. A few are. But some have economic value, and for other reasons we would be hard put to exist without them. Insects are an important food source for many animals; they are gems of natural beauty, zoological mysteries, and a constant source of interest.

WHAT INSECTS ARE   Insects are related to crabs and lobsters. Like these sea animals they possess a kind of skeleton on the *outside* of their bodies. The body itself is composed of three divisions: head, thorax, and abdomen. The thorax has three segments, each with a pair of jointed legs; so an insect normally has six legs. Most insects also have two pairs of wings attached to the thorax, but some have only one pair, and a few have none at all. Insects usually have two sets of jaws, two kinds of eyes—simple and compound—and one pair of antennae.

PARTS OF AN INSECT

antennae — jointed legs

simple eye

compound eye

head

thorax

abdomen

wings

So much for the typical insects, but many common ones are not typical. The thorax and abdomen may appear to run together. Immature stages (larvae) of many insects are worm-like, though their six true legs and perhaps some extra false ones may be counted. Immature insects are often difficult to identify. It is also hard to tell the sex of some insects. In some groups males are larger or have larger antennae or different markings. The female is sometimes marked by a spear-like ovipositor for laying eggs extending from the base of the abdomen.

INSECT RELATIVES   A number of insect-like animals are confused with insects. Spiders have only two body divisions and four pairs of legs. They have no antennae. Other insect-like animals have the head and thorax joined like the spiders. Crustaceans have at least five pairs of legs and two pairs of antennae. Most live in water (crab, lobster, shrimp), but the sowbug is a land crustacean. Centipedes and millipedes have many segments to their bodies with one pair of legs (centipedes) or two pairs (millipedes) on each. Centipedes have a pair of long antennae; millipedes have a short pair.

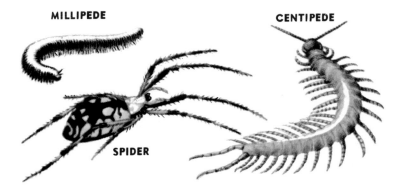

MILLIPEDE   CENTIPEDE

SPIDER

NUMBER OF INSECTS The insect group (Class Insecta) is by far the largest group of animals in the world. Over a million species have been identified, but one authority says this may be only 3 percent of the insects yet to be discovered. The class is divided into some 26 orders. One order encompasses the moths and butterflies; one, the termites; another, the beetles. The beetles alone include some 300,000 described species. There are more kinds of beetles than kinds of all other animals known, outside the insects. Butterflies and moths total over 110,000 species. Bees, wasps, and ants number 100,000; true bugs, 55,000 or more. The student of insect life need never lack material. Over 15,000 species have been found around New York City. Anyone can find a thousand species in his or her vicinity if they look for small insects as well as large, showy ones.

INSECTS AND PEOPLE Whether certain insects are considered helpful to people or otherwise, depends as much on us as it does on insects. Our ways of farming and raising animals have provided some insects which might otherwise be rare with conditions enabling them to multiply a thousandfold. Less than 1 percent of insects are harmful, but these destroy about 10 percent of our crops, causing a loss of billions of dollars annually. Some insects are parasitic on other animals, and some carry diseases.

On the other hand, this would be a sorry world without insects. We would have no apples, grapes, or clover, much less cotton, and fewer oranges and garden vegetables, for these and many other plants depend on insects to pollinate their flowers. And there would be no honey, of course. Some insects aid the process of decay, a process that is essential to life. Some insects help control others, and all help maintain a balance in nature.

INSECTS IN THEIR PLACE   In the broad view, insects play an important natural role, not only in ways that benefit man but as food for many kinds of fish, amphibians, birds, and mammals. Many of our songbirds depend almost entirely on an insect diet. Every fisherman knows how fresh-water game fish go after insects. Insects help make our rich plant life and wildlife possible. Keep this broad view in mind when people start talking about widespread insect control—something that may become possible with newer chemicals. Local control may be successful and useful to man, but control on a large scale might cause more harm than it would prevent, because insects are so important to most other kinds of life about us.

CONTROL OF INSECTS   There are ways to supplement the natural control of insects by birds and other animals. We encourage those harmless insects which prey on harmful kinds. We can exclude insects with screens, discourage them with repellents, trap them or poison them. Many of the newer poisons are highly effective. But since there are so many kinds of insects which live and feed in so many different ways, there is no single best method to get rid of them. Yet, with concerted effort some dangerous insects have been wiped out over fairly large areas. A unique example of this was the complete destruction of the Mediterranean fruit fly, which menaced the citrus crop in 20 Florida counties.

If you have an important insect problem, consult your County Agricultural Extension Agent. Often entomologists (insect specialists) at universities or museums can help, or you can turn to the U.S. Department of Agriculture's Insect Identification Laboratory, Agricultural Research Center West, Beltsville, Maryland 20705, where experts work on nearly every phase of insect life and control.

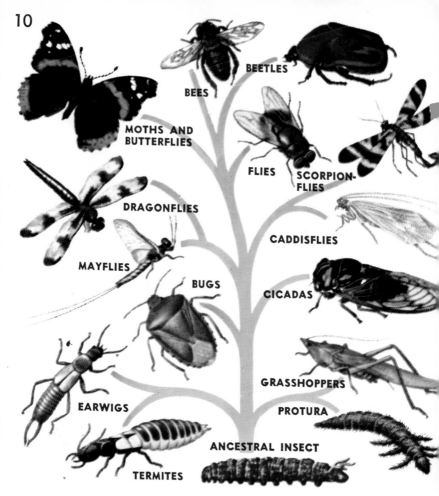

MOTHS AND
BUTTERFLIES

BEES

BEETLES

FLIES

SCORPION-
FLIES

DRAGONFLIES

CADDISFLIES

MAYFLIES

BUGS

CICADAS

EARWIGS

GRASSHOPPERS

PROTURA

ANCESTRAL INSECT

TERMITES

FAMILY TREE OF INSECTS The ancestor of all insects was probably a segmented worm-like creature much
like primitive protura, silverfish, springtails, and kin. As
long as 200 million years ago, roaches and other insects
were common. Today there are 20 to 26 orders of insects
(depending on the classification), including over one
million described species. Most of the 12,000 kinds of
fossil insects identified are similar to living species. For
relationships of insects, see "family tree" above.

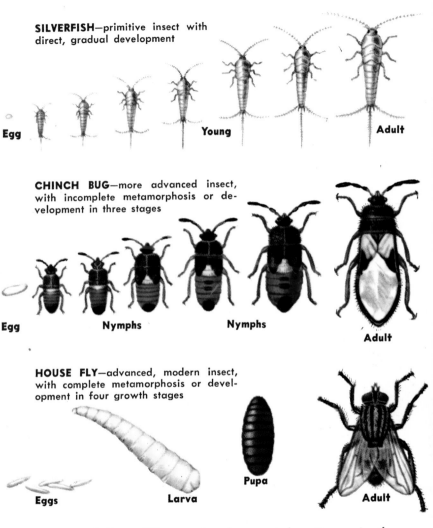

SILVERFISH—primitive insect with direct, gradual development

Egg   Young   Adult

CHINCH BUG—more advanced insect, with incomplete metamorphosis or development in three stages

Egg   Nymphs   Nymphs   Adult

HOUSE FLY—advanced, modern insect, with complete metamorphosis or development in four growth stages

Eggs   Larva   Pupa   Adult

Insects follow different developmental patterns. In the simplest, the newly hatched insect is like a miniature adult. It grows and molts (sheds its skin) till it reaches adult size. In incomplete metamorphosis an immature nymph hatches, grows, develops wings, and by stages becomes an adult. Complete metamorphosis involves (1) egg, (2) larva, (3) pupa or resting stage, (4) adult.

INTERIOR OF A GRASSHOPPER (Side View)

Heart

Blood vessel

Brain

Mouth

Anus

Digestive tract (red)

Ganglion

Gastric caeca

Nerve cord

INSECT STRUCTURE is marked by three body divisions (page 6), six jointed legs, one pair of antennae, and usually one or two pairs of wings. The outer covering, or exoskeleton, is often horny. Mouth-parts are complicated. Internally, insects possess many of the organs which are further developed in higher animals. They have a digestive tract and auxiliary digestive organs. Breathing is done by air tubes spreading internally from openings called spiracles. The head is tube-like; blood circulation is simple. Respiration, digestion, and circulation are shown in the longitudinal section (above) and cross-section (left) of the grasshopper, a typical insect.

Digestive tract

Blood vessel

Spiracle

Nerves

Air tubes

CROSS-SECTION

The nervous system (below) shows the simple brain, which exerts very little control over the body. Ganglions serve as nerve centers for nearby parts of the body.

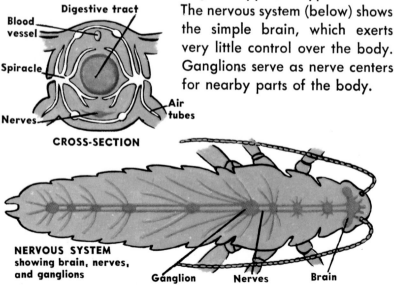

NERVOUS SYSTEM
showing brain, nerves, and ganglions

Ganglion

Nerves

Brain

HOUSE FLY—mouth for lapping

BUTTERFLY—mouth for sucking nectar

ADAPTATIONS FOR FEEDING

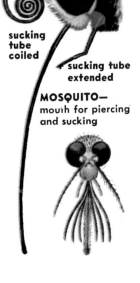

sucking tube coiled

sucking tube extended

MOSQUITO—mouth for piercing and sucking

Insect structures show vast variation. Adapted to many environments, insects live successfully in nearly every part of the world. They have digestive systems for all kinds of plant and animal food. They thrive on everything from wood to blood. A few species do not eat at all in the adult stage. Mouthparts are adapted for chewing, sucking, piercing and sucking, and lapping. Equally interesting adaptations are seen in insect wings, body coverings, and reproductive organs. The typical insect leg (as of a grasshopper) has five parts. Grasshopper hind legs are specialized for jumping. The house fly has pads which enable it to walk up windows. In honeybees, the hind leg is adapted to store and carry pollen, and the foreleg to groom and clean antennae and body. Insect structures are fascinating to study.

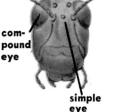

GRASSHOPPER—mouth for biting and chewing

compound eye

simple eye

ADAPTATIONS OF FEET

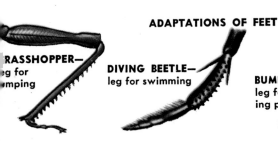

GRASSHOPPER—leg for jumping

DIVING BEETLE—leg for swimming

BUMBLEBEE—leg for carrying pollen

pollen basket

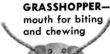

STUDYING AND COLLECTING INSECTS

Our knowledge of many insects is still so incomplete that a serious amateur can look forward to becoming a specialist doing his own scientific research.

WHERE TO LOOK Practically everywhere: in fields, gardens, woods, roadsides, beaches and swamps; under stones, rotted logs and leaves. Look in flowers, on grass; on animals, too. You'll find insects in the air; in and on water; on and in the ground.

WHEN TO LOOK Insects are most common in late summer and early fall, but experienced collectors can find them in all seasons. Some groups of insects are more common at night; remember that when collecting. In winter, concentrate on protected spots, as under stones and bark. Watch for insects in egg cases or in the resting stage (pupae).

WHAT TO DO Studying insects is not confined to catching them and mounting them in collections. Raising live insects to study their habits is exciting. Anyone can have an insect zoo in old glass jars. Collect immature insects (larvae), provide them with proper food, and watch them grow.

Watch caterpillars shed their skins, spin a cocoon or form a chrysalis, and emerge as a moth or a butterfly. See worm-like larvae become flies or beetles. Raise a colony of ants, bees, or termites. You will learn more from live insects than from dead specimens.

Whatever you do with insects, you will need some understanding of what insects are and how they live. Use this book, then read some of the other books suggested. Most important, go out and look at insects. Catch them if you wish, but watch them first. See how they move, how they feed, and what they do.

COLLECTING INSECTS An insect collection can be valuable for study or reference—if it is used. Using a collection means more than making a collection, though this step must come first. Fortunately, beginners can collect insects with simple, low-cost equipment. Not all insects are chased with a net. Hang an old bedsheet out at night with a small light in front of it. Roll the bottom into a funnel, with a jar set beneath. Insects hitting the sheet will roll down into the jar. Similar traps are described in reference books. Try the easiest methods and places first—as your window screens or near a large neon sign. Just gather the insect harvest there.

EQUIPMENT Any large, wide-mouthed jar will serve for confining and raising insects. Tie some gauze or netting over the top. To kill specimens use a wide-mouthed bottle with absorbent cotton or sawdust on the bottom, wet with a tablespoon or so of carbon tetrachloride or carbona. Cover this with a sheet of tight-fitting cardboard punched full of pinholes. Because cyanide is such a dangerous poison, cyanide bottles should be made and used only by experienced collectors. A light net with a long handle is good for catching insects on the wing. A heavier net is better for "sweeping" through the grass or for catching water insects.

Cigar boxes with a layer of heavy corrugated cardboard on the bottom to hold pins are fine for storing specimens. Use a mothball to deter insect pests. Purchase and use insect pins; ordinary ones are too heavy. Learn the tricks that make mounting neat and attractive. A book for records is essential; so are labels. Later you may want spreading boards, pinning blocks, and other accessories. Collecting and preserving specimens requires real skill. Read first; then practice with any insects you may find in your own yard. Skill will come with experience.

FIELD AND LIFE-HISTORY STUDIES may prove more interesting and exciting than collecting. Instead of learning a little about many insects, learn a lot about a few. Field studies can involve unusual problems on which there is little or no scientific information. How do ants recognize one another? How does temperature affect the flight of butterflies? How much does a caterpillar eat? Can beetles recognize color? Such problems can be investigated in your own yard if you are interested. Many insects are known only in the adult form; few facts are known about the rest of their life cycles. Constant observation of wild specimens, or detailed study of captive ones reared under natural conditions, may yield many new and interesting facts.

WALKINGSTICK
3.0"

black locust

WALKINGSTICKS are large, usually wingless insects with legs all about the same length, distinguishing them from the mantises (pp. 24-25). Walkingsticks live and feed on leaves of oak, locust, cherry, and walnut, occasionally causing damage. The female's 100 or so eggs are dropped singly to the ground to hatch the following spring. As young grow, they molt or shed their skin five or six times; otherwise they are similar to adults. Males are smaller than females.

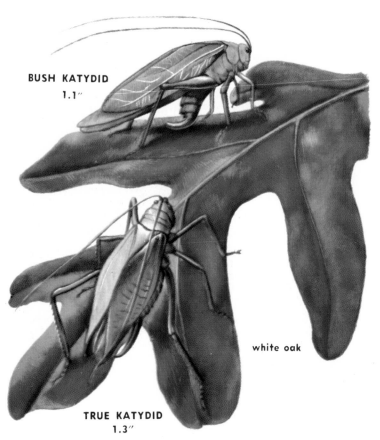

BUSH KATYDID
1.1"

white oak

TRUE KATYDID
1.3"

KATYDIDS The male of the true katydid makes the persistent "katydid" call, which is an accepted part of a summer's evening. At the base of the outer wings or wing-covers of the males are rasps and ridges which, when rubbed like a fiddle and bow, produce the calls of different species. Katydids hear by "ears" on the upper part of their front legs. Some katydids are tree dwellers, feeding on leaves of cherry, oak, maple, and apple. Others live in weeds and shrubs. Most are green, with thin, leaf-like

**ANGULAR-
WINGED
KATYDID
1.1"**

eggs

wing-covers, and so have the advantage of protective coloration. However, some species are brown or even pink. All have long antennae. Females, recognized by the long ovipositor, usually place 100-150 oval eggs on leaves or twigs early in the fall. When young emerge in spring, they resemble their parents, but are much smaller, lighter in color, and lack wings. In the South, two broods are produced each season.

True Katydid

MOLE
CRICKET
1.3"

CAMEL CRICKET   0.8"

MOLE AND CAMEL CRICKETS These nocturnal crickets live under rocks in moist places, or mostly underground. The large mole cricket burrows near the surface, eating young roots and killing seedlings. In the South, it destroys peanuts, strawberries, and other garden crops. The pale brown, spotted, wingless camel (or cave) cricket is identified by its high, arched back. Though a scavenger, it often becomes a nuisance around greenhouses.

Mole Cricket

MORMON CRICKET
female 1.5"   male smaller

wheat

MORMON CRICKET This serious pest of Western grains and other crops is partly controlled by insect parasites, small mammals, and birds. Gulls saved the crops of the early Mormon settlers from hordes of these crickets which descended upon them. The large, clumsy insects devour everything in their path, including each other. Some Western Indians considered them a delicacy and ate them roasted. Small clusters of eggs are laid in the ground by the female.

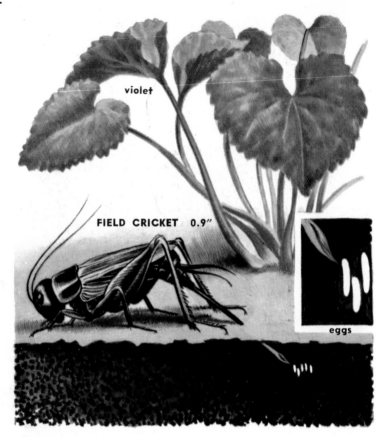

violet

FIELD CRICKET 0.9"

eggs

FIELD CRICKETS These common, large-headed, black or brown crickets are largely nocturnal. Their shrill musical song is made by rubbing the forewings. Though vegetarians, they may eat other insects and each other. Field crickets occasionally damage crops and invade homes, even eating clothing. Eggs are laid in the ground in fall. The young nymphs emerge in spring and develop their adult wings in several stages by late summer. Several species, all similar in appearance, are found here.

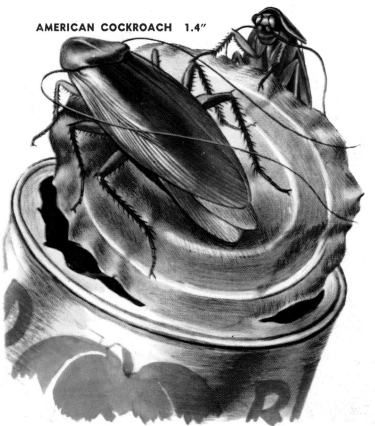

AMERICAN COCKROACH 1.4"

AMERICAN COCKROACH The common roach, bane of homemakers, traces its ancestry back to the Coal Age. This large brown species is most common in the South. Some kinds live in houses and barns, others in fields. They eat all kinds of food and sometimes destroy books, rugs, and clothing. They prefer moist, dark places and usually come out at night. This roach differs from the smaller German roach (pp. 152-153). The American roach is probably native to our tropics.

CAROLINA
MANTIS
2.3"

egg cases

MANTISES These large, slender insects, generally called praying mantises or mantids, are predators, feeding mainly on other insects. If confined, mantises are likely to turn cannibal. They are colored a protective green or brown. Hard to see on foliage, they wait in ambush, snatching passing insects with their spiny forelegs. Mantids use their exceptional powers of vision and ability to rotate their heads to detect the movements of prey.

In fall, after mating, the female may eat the male.

PRAYING MANTIS 3.5"

egg case

She lays several hundred eggs in a frothy mass that dries like hardened brown foam. Egg cases can be found in the winter and brought indoors to hatch. The young, similar to adults but light yellow, are difficult to raise.

The Carolina mantis is smaller than the others. It is one of 20 native species found most commonly in the South. The Chinese and European mantises, introduced here more than 50 years ago, are abundant throughout the East.

Carolina

AMERICAN GRASSHOPPER 2.0"

goldenrod

CAROLINA GRASSHOPPER 1.2"

GRASSHOPPERS AND LOCUSTS are a group of closely related insects. Some species migrate; others do not. All are similar, with short antennae and large hearing organs on the abdomen. Most are good fliers, though some kinds are wingless. Locusts and grasshoppers sometimes destroy crops, especially in the West, where they are more common; but they serve as food for larger birds, small mammals, and other animals. Females lay 20 to 100 eggs in the ground or in rotted wood. See p. 28 for the life history of one species. Nymphs mature in 2 to 3 months.

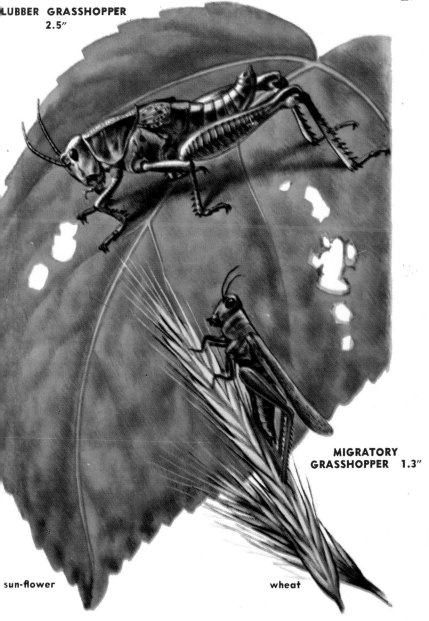

LUBBER GRASSHOPPER
2.5"

MIGRATORY
GRASSHOPPER 1.3"

sun-flower   wheat

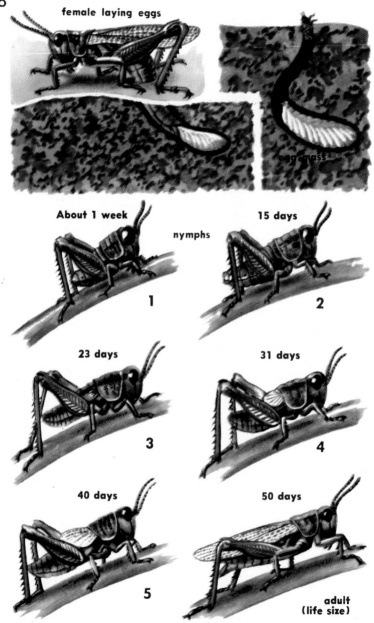

female laying eggs

egg mass

About 1 week

nymphs

15 days

1

2

23 days

31 days

3

4

40 days

50 days

5

adult
(life size)

RED-LEGGED GRASSHOPPER

EUROPEAN
EARWIG 0.6"

EARWIGS have short, leathery forewings and a pincer-like abdominal appendage. From their abdominal glands earwigs exude a liquid with a tar-like odor. They are nocturnal, spending the day in crevices or damp places. The legend of their creeping into ears of sleeping persons is untrue. Although several species occur in North America, the most widespread is the introduced European Earwig. It feeds on dead organic matter, fungi, pollen, and plants in addition to insect prey.

European Earwig

Seaside Earwig

soldier

queen

eggs

TERMITES Though sometimes called white ants, termites are not ants, and some are not white. Of some 2,000 species, only about 40 are found in this country. Many more are tropical. These highly socialized insects live in colonies composed of four distinct castes. The king and the queen, and the winged termites which can become kings and queens of new colonies, form the first caste. The enlarged and almost helpless queen produces thousands upon thousands of eggs. Most of these hatch into whitish, blind workers who make up the second caste.

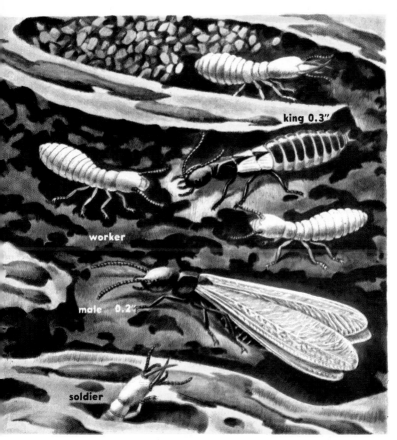

Soldiers with large heads and jaws, and nymphs, which take over the task of reproduction should the king or queen die, make up the last two castes.

With the aid of protozoa living in their digestive tracts, termites feed on wood and do some one billion dollars worth of damage annually to buildings in this country. The young pass through six stages as they develop into adults. Tropical termites build huge nests or mounds, often higher than a man.

HEAD LOUSE 0.1"

egg

SHORT-NOSED CATTLE LOUSE 0.1+"   **CRAB LOUSE 0.1—"**   **BODY LOUSE 0.1+"**

LICE are minute, wingless insects that live and breed on their hosts. All are parasites; some carry disease. Biting lice (bird lice), a distinct group, feed on hair, feathers, and fragments of skin. The sucking lice take the host's blood directly, by means of sucking mouth-parts. The hog lice (¼ in.) are the largest of this group. The head louse infects humans and is known to carry typhus, trench fever, and relapsing fever. Six to 12 generations of lice may mature annually. Young, similar to adults, develop rapidly.

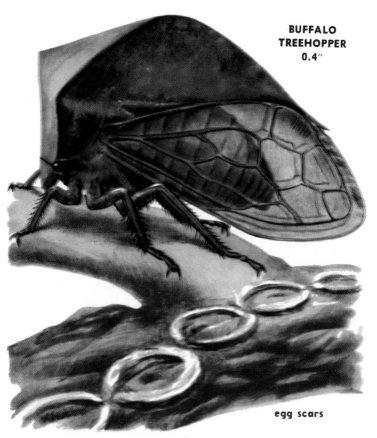

BUFFALO
TREEHOPPER
0.4"

egg scars

TREEHOPPERS The common green and brown tree-hoppers are small, winged, sucking insects of curious and peculiar shapes. They live on many plants, feeding on the sap. Because of their protective color and form, they are usually noticed only when moving. Nearly 200 species are known in this country, many with bizarre shapes. Eggs are laid in stems and buds, sometimes causing minor damage. Eggs hatch the following spring. Young are similar to adults.

RED-BANDED LEAFHOPPER 0.3"

LATERAL LEAFHOPPER 0.4"

LEAFHOPPERS These attractive, slender, multicolored insects are often abundant on plants where they can feed by sucking the sap. This causes wilting and injury to grape, apple, clover, beet, and other plants. Besides, leafhoppers sometimes carry virus diseases from plant to plant and thus become serious pests.

Leafhoppers exude "honeydew" as they feed. This is a somewhat sweet surplus sap which attracts ants and bees, which feed on it. Leafhoppers are well known as prodigious jumpers. They are sometimes called dodgers

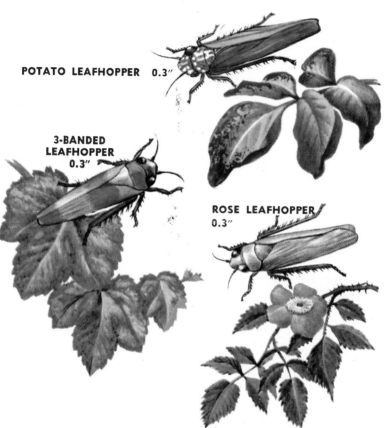

POTATO LEAFHOPPER 0.3"

3-BANDED
LEAFHOPPER
0.3"

ROSE LEAFHOPPER
0.3"

because of the way they slip out of sight when disturbed.

The female lays eggs in stems and leaves. Two or more generations are produced each year. Late eggs winter over and hatch in spring. Adults hibernate and emerge in spring also. The young pass through 4 to 5 nymph stages before they mature. Leafhopper populations in fields may reach as high as a million per acre. Of some 10,000 known species, about 2,800 are found in the United States.

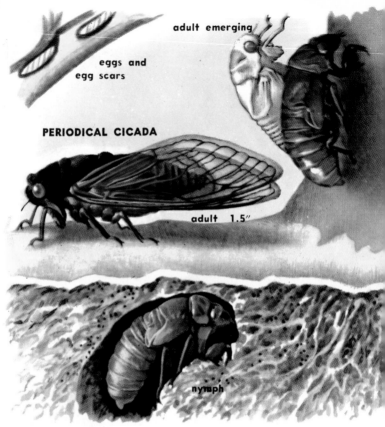

eggs and
egg scars

adult emerging

PERIODICAL CICADA

adult 1.5"

nymph

CICADAS, whose steady hum fills the late summer air, are more often heard than seen. Males make the sharp sound with plate-like organs on the thorax. Some species are called harvestflies because of their late summer appearance; others are called 13-year and 17-year locusts, though the 75 species of cicadas differ widely in the time they take to mature. The females cut slits in young twigs and deposit eggs in them. This sometimes causes damage in nurseries and orchards, because the slit twigs break easily in the wind. As the wingless, scaly

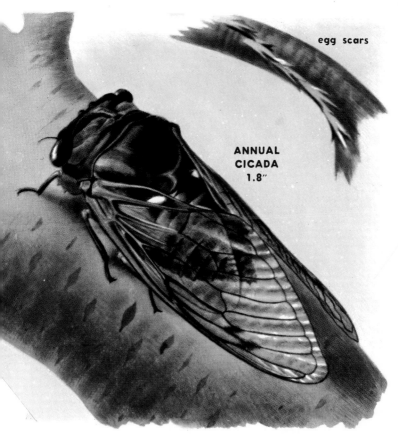

egg scars

**ANNUAL
CICADA
1.8″**

young hatch, they drop to the ground, burrow in, and stay there 4 to 20 years (depending on the species and the latitude) as nymphs living on juices sucked from roots. The full-grown nymph climbs a tree trunk. The skin splits down the back; the adult emerges. In most species, adults ordinarily live a few weeks—long enough to mate and lay eggs. "Broods" or large colonies of periodical (13- and 17-year) cicadas emerge en masse, and many are eaten by birds.

Periodical

Annual   13-year

38

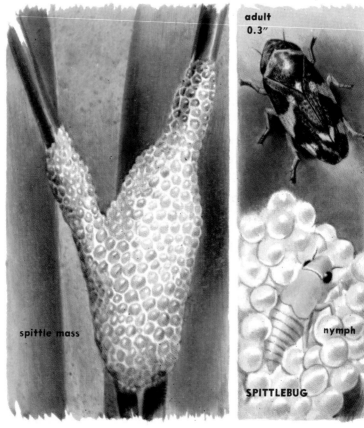

adult
0.3"

spittle mass

nymph

SPITTLEBUG

SPITTLEBUG   Female spittlebugs make a froth on stems and grasses to cover their eggs. The young nymphs make a froth also to cover themselves while feeding. Open the small mass of bubbles and you are likely to see the small, dull, squat insect inside. Spittlebugs are also called froghoppers because the adults hop about from plant to plant and seldom fly. Though spittlebugs are of minor importance, some kinds injure pine trees and various garden plants.

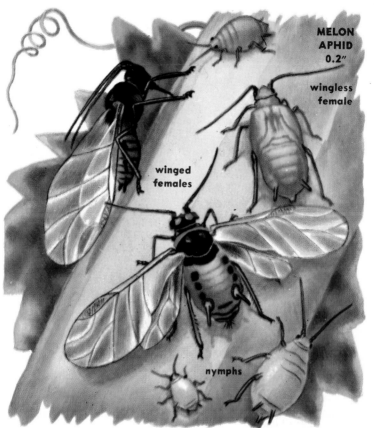

MELON
APHID
0.2″

winged
females

wingless
female

nymphs

APHIDS are minute sucking insects, wingless or with transparent or colored wings. They are abundant on many plants, causing damage by sucking juices or transmitting virus diseases as they feed. Some form and live in galls. Most have complicated life histories. Only wingless females emerge from the eggs in spring. These produce generations of females all summer—sometimes a dozen. Winged females develop in the fall. Their young are normal males and females, which, after mating, produce the eggs from which new aphids emerge in spring.

TERRAPIN
SCALE
0.1"

SAN JOSE SCALE 0.1"

SCALE INSECTS are a large group of small sucking insects. Individually minute, these insects live in colonies which often cover branches, twigs, and leaves of the plants on which they feed by sucking juices. Species differ markedly in appearance. Many have a scale-like covering and are immobile when mature. Other species lack scales, but are covered with a "honeydew" secretion eaten by bees and ants. These species move very little. Legs are poorly developed. Males are smaller and differ from the females; when mature they have small wings.

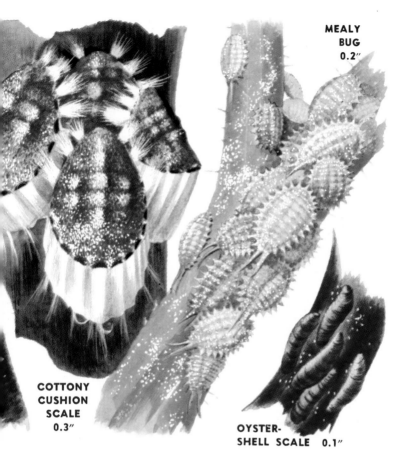

MEALY BUG 0.2"

COTTONY CUSHION SCALE 0.3"

OYSTER-SHELL SCALE 0.1"

Scale insects attack and injure citrus, apple, and other fruit trees, and greenhouse and ornamental plants. Scales are difficult to control. Ladybugs, certain small wasps, and other natural enemies are used in fighting them.

Reproduction is complicated. Most scale insects spend the winter as eggs, which the female deposits under her shell before she dies. The eggs hatch in spring and the young move to fresh growth before they settle down under a scale. Some species produce several generations of females before normal sexual reproduction takes place.

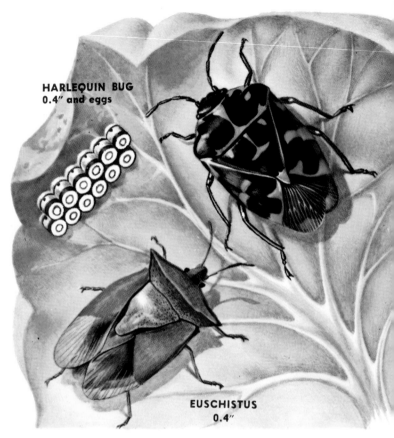

HARLEQUIN BUG
0.4" and eggs

EUSCHISTUS
0.4"

STINK BUGS AND SHIELD BUGS There are several hundred species of stink bugs and shield bugs in this country. All have the flattened, shield-shaped body. Most suck plant juices but some feed on other insects. Most are colored green or brown, to match their environment, and are not easily noticed. A black species common on blackberries and raspberries is so well concealed it is sometimes eaten. The colorful harlequin bug is an exception, even to its unusual eggs. The young, hatching from the eggs, pass through a series of growth stages till the nymphs

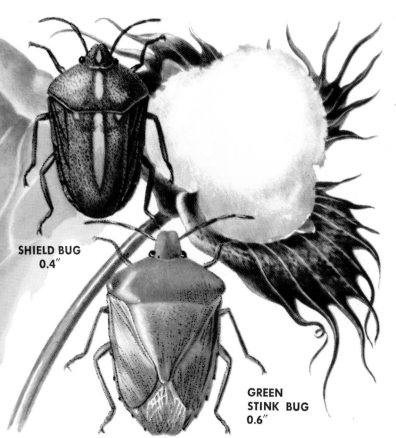

SHIELD BUG
0.4"

GREEN
STINK BUG
0.6"

become adults. The odor, which comes from two glands on the thorax and which gives stink bugs their name, is also characteristic of a number of other bugs. Birds are not bothered by the odor and commonly feed on the insects. The harlequin bug and several other species are destructive to garden crops. The shield bugs are very similar to stink bugs. In these species, the shield, which develops from the thorax, is so large that it covers a good part of the abdomen.

Stink Bugs
and Shield Bugs

Harlequin Bug
more common

SQUASH BUG 0.6"

TACHINID FLY 0.4"

SQUASH BUGS cause considerable damage to squash, pumpkins, gourds, and related crops by sucking juices from leaves and stems of young plants. The bugs have a strong, offensive odor. Eggs, laid in late spring, hatch in about 2 weeks. The attractive nymph is green, soon turning brown or gray. Adults hibernate over the winter. A tachinid fly, which lays its eggs in nymphs and adult squash bugs, parasitizes these pests and helps reduce their numbers.

SMALL MILKWEED
BUG 0.4"

LARGE
MILKWEED
BUG 0.5"

MILKWEED BUGS These black and red or orange bugs are similar and closely related to the tiny destructive chinch bug (p. 47). About 200 species are grouped in the same family with the milkweed bugs, but most are much smaller and less attractive in color and pattern. Milkweed bugs feed on all varieties of milkweed and are of no economic importance. Adults which hibernate over the winter produce young in late spring. The nymphs mature and breed by late summer.

Small

Large

AMBUSH BUG 0.4"
feeding on aphid

AMBUSH BUG   These small, oddly shaped predators form a minor group of some 25 species. Their habit is to lie concealed in flowers, grasping any small insects which may come by. Their front legs are modified for holding their victims; the mouth, for tearing and sucking. Interesting because of their bizarre forms and feeding habits, the ambush bugs lack economic importance. Not common enough to control injurious insects, they do eat beneficial ones also.

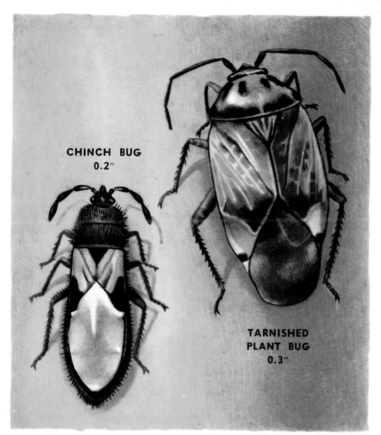

CHINCH BUG
0.2"

TARNISHED
PLANT BUG
0.3"

CHINCH BUG Though small, almost minute, chinch bugs reproduce so rapidly they overrun grain fields, destroying the crops as they feed on plant juices. The annual damage in this country runs into millions. About 500 eggs are deposited in grass or grain. Nymphs are red, becoming gray or brown with age. Two or three generations may develop in one season. The tarnished plant bug, somewhat larger, and of a related family, is destructive to many kinds of fruits.

Chinch Bug

BACKSWIMMER
0.5"

**WATER-
BOATMAN
0.4"**

AQUATIC BUGS are found in nearly every pond and stream. A few species are marine also. All are remarkable for their adaptations to life on or below the surface. Nearly all are predaceous, attacking other insects, snails, small fish, etc. In turn, these insects are food for larger fish and water birds. The water striders, taking advantage of surface tension on water, stay on the surface without breaking through. They skate along with remarkable speed. Other water bugs spend most of their time under water. Some carry down air on the surface of their bodies

TER STRIDERS 0.4"

GIANT WATER
BUG 2.2"

and use this for respiration. Other species breathe air that
is dissolved in the water. In most cases, the young resemble
the adults and mature after a series of nymphal stages.
The water-boatmen have an erratic swimming pattern.
The backswimmers, as their name indicates, swim on their
backs, but can also fly. The giant water bugs, sometimes 2
inches or more in length, prefer quiet water. Since their
bite can produce a painful swelling, the amateur collector
should exercise caution. When abundant these giant water
bugs are harmful in fish hatcheries.

GREEN DARNER
2.6"

nymph

DRAGONFLIES AND DAMSELFLIES are often seen near ponds and moist meadows, but some species dwell in forests. Dragonflies, also known as darning needles or stingers, are reputed to be dangerous. They are, but only to small insects, like mosquitoes, which they eat on the wing. Dragonflies rest with wings outstretched. The more delicate damselfly rests with wings folded. Both lay eggs in water; the nymphs develop there, feeding on other aquatic insects. They leave the water after several growing stages; the skin splits and the adult emerges.

**TEN-SPOT
DRAGONFLY
2.0″**

cast
skin

arrowhead

**BLACKWING
DAMSELFLY 1.3″**

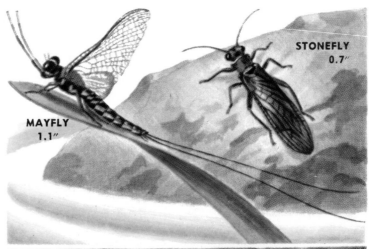

MAYFLIES AND STONEFLIES are unrelated (p. 4) yet are similarly adapted to aquatic environments. The 100 or so species of mayflies have transparent, veined wings and a long, forked tail. Myriads of short-lived adults are seen on mating flights or near lights. The stoneflies include some 200 species. The nymphs, like those of mayflies, live in water and are important food of fresh-water fish. Both nymphs take several years to reach the adult stage. Adult stoneflies have transparent wings, but do not fly very much or very often.

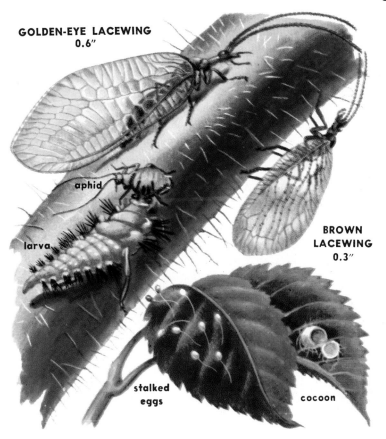

GOLDEN-EYE LACEWING
0.6"

aphid

larva

BROWN
LACEWING
0.3"

stalked
eggs

cocoon

LACEWINGS serve a double natural function. The adults
are sometimes eaten by birds. The larvae feed on aphids
and other destructive insects, earning the name aphid
lions. Many of the larvae of the 20 or more kinds of brown
lacewings cover themselves with remains of aphids and
other debris. The female Golden-eye lacewing lays
stalked eggs which the larvae some-
times eat. Larvae spin silky cocoons
from which they emerge as delicate,
thin-winged adults.

54

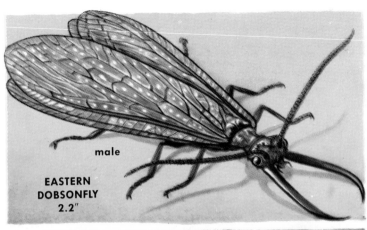

male

EASTERN
DOBSONFLY
2.2"

larva

DOBSONFLY The ferocious-looking adult male is harmless. The long mandibles are used in the mating, which ends its short life. The female lacks these exaggerated mouth-parts. She lays a mass of thousands of eggs on plants overhanging a pond or stream. The larvae emerge, drop into the water, and spend the next three years feeding on smaller water life. Fishermen prize the large larvae, called hellgrammites, as live bait.

ANT LION 1.1"

larva 0.7"

ANT LIONS are so named because the larvae of members of this family have odd feeding habits. Eggs are laid on the ground. When one hatches, the larva digs a pit in sand or sandy soil and lives almost completely buried at the bottom. Should an ant or other small insect tumble in, it is seized in powerful jaws and sucked dry. As the larva, or "doodlebug," matures, it builds a silken cocoon, in which it pupates. The adult resembles a miniature, drab damselfly with short antennae.

SCORPIONFLY
0.6"

SCORPIONFLIES are not poisonous, and resemble scorpions only in the modified tips of their abdomens. Eggs are deposited in the soil, where they develop into larvae. The larvae change into pupae, from which the fly-like adults emerge to live as scavengers, feeding on dead or disabled insects. Adults are found on plants. They do not fly well or often. One group of small, almost wingless scorpionflies live in northern woods and are active even on snow in winter.

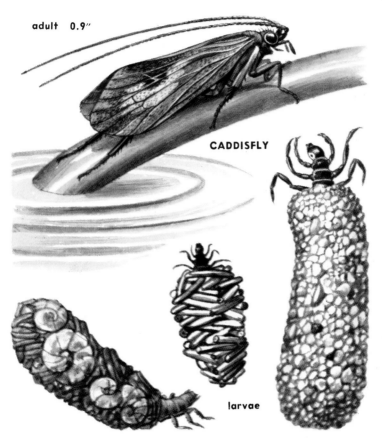

adult 0.9"

CADDISFLY

larvae

CADDISFLIES include 17 families and over 200 species. The unusual larvae, so common in fresh water, are best known. These build cases of sand or plant debris, cemented together by silk. Cases built by different species are distinctive. After the adults mate in flights over the water, the female lays several hundred eggs on submerged rocks or plants. Larvae feed on small water plants and animals, and in turn are food of many fish. Larvae pupate in the larval case.

antennae of butterfly (left) and moth

BUTTERFLIES AND MOTHS   The largest, most attractive, and best-known insects are grouped together in the order Lepidoptera, the butterflies and moths. The

scales of butterflies

order includes 65 families of moths and 5 of butterflies. About 12,000 species are known in North America. All, except very few, have two pairs of wings. These and the body are covered with scales

or modified hairs, which give moths and butterflies their color. The mouth-parts of adults form a sucking tube which is rolled into a tight coil when not in use.

Lepidoptera have four stages of development: egg, larva (caterpillar), pupa (cocoon or chrysalis), and adult. Most butterfly eggs are laid singly or a few at a time and are unprotected. Many moths lay a large number of eggs in one place and may cover the egg mass with a

protective coating which includes hairs and scales from the female's body. There is no rule of thumb for distinguishing caterpillars of moths

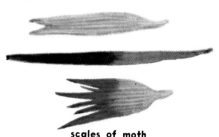

scales of moth

GIANT SWALLOWTAIL
caterpillar

from those of butterflies. Both have chewing mouthparts, primarily for feeding on plants. A handful of species sometimes do tremendous damage to crops. Most caterpillars have 6 true legs on the thorax, and from 4 to 10 unjointed false legs on the abdomen. A few have irritating hairs or spines. Many caterpillars spin a silken cocoon, sometimes covered with hairs, in which they pupate. Butterfly larvae make no cocoon but form a chrysalis. Some Lepidoptera winter as pupae, others as eggs or caterpillars, and a few as adults.

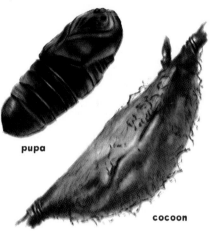

pupa

cocoon

The adult moth and butterfly are usually quite different, though one group, the skippers, shows intermediate characteristics. Butterflies usually fly by day; moths ordinarily fly by night. The former customarily rest with their wings folded back; moths rest with their wings in a horizontal position. The antennae of butterflies are thin, ending in a knob. Those of moths never end in knobs and are often feathery. Though some butterflies are more attractive, the moths form a larger, more diverse, and more important group.

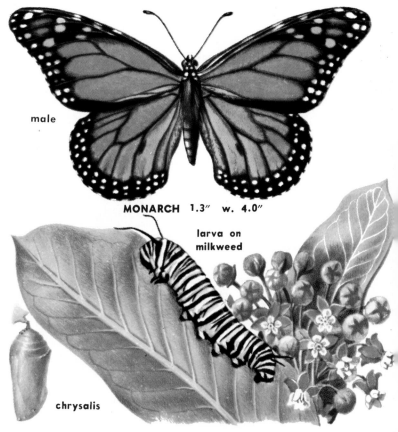

male

MONARCH 1.3″ w. 4.0″

larva on
milkweed

chrysalis

MONARCH This is a common and attractive butterfly. Males are identified by a black scent pocket on the
third vein of the hindwing. Two or three generations
grow in one summer. In fall, swarms of adults migrate
southward to California and Mexico, covering entire
trees when they stop to rest. They do not hibernate, as
is sometimes believed. Adults are
often distasteful to birds, the result
of feeding as caterpillars on milk-
weeds, which contain natural
poisons.

larva on poplar

VICEROY
1.0″ w. 2.8″

VICEROY This butterfly resembles the monarch in wing color, pattern, flight, and some habits. It, too, is abundant in late summer. But the viceroy is smaller and has curved black lines crossing the veins of the hindwings. Its eggs, and the larvae which feed on poplar and willow, resemble those of the purples (p. 62), to which the viceroy is related. Partly-grown larvae hibernate in rolled leaves for the winter. There are two generations or more a year.

62

BANDED
PURPLE
1.0" w. 2.9"

RED-SPOTTED
PURPLE
1.0"
w. 3.1"

PURPLES   The banded purple has a conspicuous white band across its wings with a border of red and blue spots on the hindwings. Eggs are laid on leaves of willow, birch, and poplar, on which the larvae feed. The red-spotted purple is so named for its red spots on the under side along the wing borders and at the base of the hindwings. The larvae feed on wild cherry, willow, and other trees, preferring shaded woods.

BUCKEYE
0.8″   w. 2.5″

larva

plantain

BUCKEYE   Though it is most common in the South and West, the buckeye is occasionally found in the North. The eye-spots make identification of the butterfly easy. The buckeye lays its green, ribbed eggs chiefly on plantain, snapdragon, and ruellia, and it is on these plants that its larvae feed. The larva forms a brown chrysalis from which the adult eventually emerges. Buckeyes are medium-sized butterflies. They are often found in open fields. In the South there are two similar species, with smaller eye-spots on the hindwings.

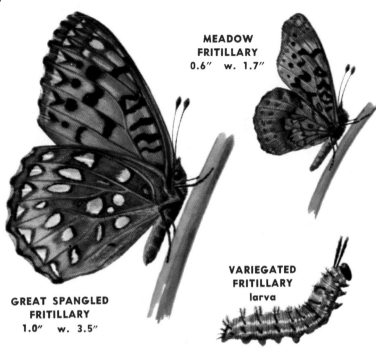

**MEADOW
FRITILLARY
0.6"   w. 1.7"**

**GREAT SPANGLED
FRITILLARY
1.0"   w. 3.5"**

**VARIEGATED
FRITILLARY
larva**

**REGAL
FRITILLARY
1.0"
w. 3.4"**

upper side

GULF FRITILLARY
0.9″ w. 2.9″

SILVER-BORDERED FRITILLARY
0.6″ w. 1.5″

GULF FRITILLARY larva

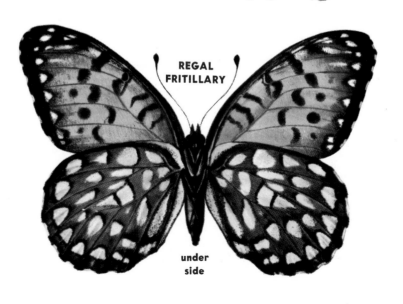

REGAL FRITILLARY

under side

FRITILLARIES The fritillaries, one of the largest groups of butterflies, are found not only in this country but in many other parts of the world as well. The family of which they are the most important members has front legs which are reduced in size and held close to the body. Only 4 of the 6 legs are used in walking. Fritillaries are mostly medium-sized butterflies, orange or reddish above, with silvery or light spots on the underside of the hindwings. Sometimes the males are a brighter red on top than the females.

The different species of fritillaries are distinct enough to make general statements about them difficult. The eggs are generally barrel-shaped and ornamented with ridges. All the caterpillars are spiny, with the spines on the head a bit longer than the others. Most feed at night on such plants as violets, goldenrods, and other composites. While the early stages of the common fritillaries are known, there are many less common species, and information on the egg and caterpillar of these species is incomplete. The chrysalis of fritillaries is usually angular, forked at the top, and bordered with knobs. It is often brownish.

Of the many fritillaries, those illustrated are among the most common and best known. The Gulf fritillary belongs to a different group from the others and is not considered a "true" fritillary.

GREAT SPANGLED FRITILLARY larva

CHALCEDON
CHECKERSPOT
0.5″ w. 1.6″

turtlehead

BALTIMORE
0.7″ w. 1.9″

CHECKERSPOTS This is a group of small, attractive butterflies. The Baltimore is common locally and occurs in June, usually in boggy areas where its principal plant food, turtlehead, grows. The caterpillar is black with orange bands and shiny black spines. The wing pattern of the chalcedon checkerspot varies considerably throughout its range. The caterpillar is black with orange spots at the base of the spines. It feeds on painted cups and monkey flowers, which are common in the West.

Baltimore

Chalcedon

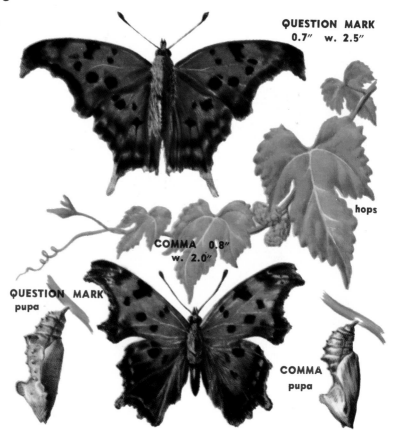

QUESTION MARK
0.7″ w. 2.5″

hops

COMMA 0.8″
w. 2.0″

QUESTION MARK
pupa

COMMA
pupa

ANGLE WINGS This group of small to medium-sized butterflies has angular, notched forewings. The hindwings often have short tails. Of 25 species found in this country, the question mark (also called the violet-tip), comma, and mourning cloak are best known. The brownish larvae of the question mark feed on hops, elm, and nettle. The greenish, often pale comma caterpillar feeds on nettles. Both caterpillars have branched spines on each body segment and the head.

Comma

Question Mark

MOURNING CLOAK
1.0″ w. 2.6″

larva

chrysalis

elm

eggs

MOURNING CLOAK   This butterfly, like other angle wings, hibernates as an adult and hence makes its appearance very early in spring. Dark, barrel-shaped eggs are soon laid on twigs of poplar, elm, hackberry, or willow. The gregarious black, spiny caterpillars occasionally injure small trees by stripping the foliage. The mourning cloak is common and widely distributed over the entire northern hemisphere. In the North it has one brood a year; in the South, two.

70

AMERICAN PAINTED LADY
(HUNTER'S BUTTERFLY)
0.8" w. 2.0"

RED ADMIRAL
0.8" w. 2.0"

larva on
nettle

RED ADMIRAL, AMERICAN PAINTED LADY, and PAINTED LADY Two of these three closely related butterflies are difficult to distinguish. But the red admiral is clear and unmistakable because of the red bands on its forewings and red borders on its hindwings. The red admiral is found the world around in the northern hemisphere. The light green eggs are barrel-shaped. The caterpillar feeds on hops, ramie, and nettles. American painted lady is restricted to North America. Its upper side is very similar to that of the painted lady. The under side is distinct

PAINTED LADY
0.8″ w. 2.2″

thistle

in having two large "eye-spots" which the painted lady lacks. The American's larvae are spiny and black, with rows of white spots. It feeds on arrowweed, cudweed, and other everlastings. The painted lady or thistle butterfly is reported to be the most widely distributed of all known butterflies. This may be because burdock, thistles, sunflowers, nettles, and other plants which larvae eat are widely distributed also. Caterpillar is greenish, with black spots and light, branched spines.

Red Admiral and Painted Lady

Amer. Painted Lady

NORTHERN EYED BROWN
0.6″   w. 1.8″

PEARLY-EYE and larva
0.7″   w. 2.0″

NYMPHS AND SATYRS   About 60 species make up this large group of small to medium-sized butterflies, most of which are dull brownish or gray in color. Their characteristic markings are eye-spots on the undersides of the wings. Most prefer open woods and mountain areas, generally in the north. The green caterpillars of these species are smooth, and taper toward both the head and the tail, which is always forked. The larvae of the eyed brown have a pair of red horns at each end. Their food is primarily sedge and other grasses. Pearly-

COMMON WOOD NYMPH
0.8" w. 2.0"

LITTLE WOOD SATYR
0.7" w. 1.8"

eyes are slightly larger in size, and their larvae similar in appearance. The common wood nymph has a pair of yellow patches on each forewing surrounding the purplish eye-spots. The male has two small eye-spots on the hindwings. Markings vary a good deal. The larvae lack the horns of the first two species. The little wood satyr is smaller, with eye-spots on both fore- and hindwings. The larva has no red at all; color varies from greenish to pale brown.

Wood Nymph

Pearly Eyes (3 species)

GRAY HAIRSTREAK
0.4" w. 1.2"

PURPLISH COPPER
0.5" w. 1.2"

AMERICAN COPPER
0.4" w. 1.0"

BRONZE COPPER
0.5" w. 1.5"

COPPERS AND BLUES This large family of small butterflies includes over 2,000 species, but not many species are found in this country. These butterflies are common. The family has three groups. The hairstreaks are usually brownish or bluish, with hair-like tails at the tip of the hindwings. About 60 species of hairstreaks live in the United States. The second group, the coppers, are nearly all a copper-red color with black markings. There are some 18 species. The American copper is probably our most common butterfly. It is found everywhere east of the Rockies. The last group, the blues, are very small. Western

**EASTERN
TAILED
BLUE
0.4"
w. 1.0"**

**SPRING AZURE
0.4"   w. 1.1"**

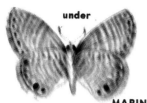

under

**MARINE BLUE
0.4"   w. 1.1"**

upper

**WESTERN PYGMY BLUE
0.2"   w. 0.6"**

pygmy blue is our smallest butterfly. Blues are more common in the West. Some 40 species, variable in form and difficult to identify, are listed for the United States. The spring azure has over 13 different variations. The caterpillars of all this family are short, thick, and slug-like. Some are flattened and covered with fine hair. They feed on a variety of plants, principally legumes, but also oak, hickory, hops, and sorrel. One species, the harvester, has a carnivorous caterpillar which devours plant lice.

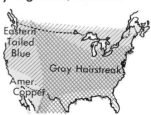

Eastern Tailed Blue

Gray Hairstreak

Amer. Copper

76

CABBAGE BUTTERFLY
0.7″ w. 1.8″

larva

chrysalis

CABBAGE BUTTERFLY This all-too-common species ranges over most of the northern hemisphere. It first entered this country in 1868 and within 20 years had spread to the Rockies. Now these insects are found in every cabbage field; the green caterpillars feed also on mustard and related wild plants. Two or three broods mature each year, the last brood hibernating as the chrysalis and emerging in early spring. Adults often fly in flocks of a dozen or two.

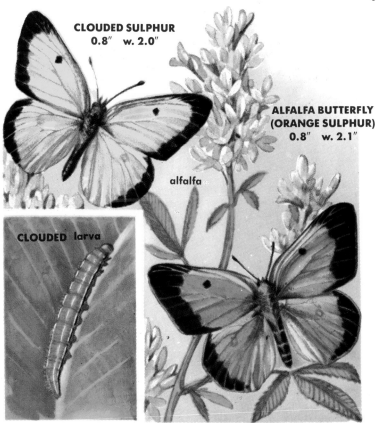

CLOUDED SULPHUR
0.8" w. 2.0"

**ALFALFA BUTTERFLY
(ORANGE SULPHUR)**
0.8" w. 2.1"

alfalfa

CLOUDED larva

SULPHURS Dozens of common or clouded sulphurs cluster together over roadside puddles. Their color is variable; females are paler, with yellow spots in borders of forewings. There are two generations annually. The alfalfa butterfly, also varying in color, is sometimes pale. It also is common along roadsides, in fields and gardens. The larva is similar to the common sulphur's, but has pink stripes. Both these larvae feed on clover, alfalfa, and other legumes.

Alfalfa Butterfly

Clouded Sulphur

78

SPICEBUSH SWALLOWTAIL
0.8″ w. 3.5″

PARNASSIUS
0.8″ w. 2.4″

GIANT SWALLOWTAIL
1.0″ w. 4.4″

ZEBRA SWALLOWTAIL
0.8″ w. 2.7″

BLACK SWALLOWTAIL   0.8″ w. 2.8″

TIGER SWALLOWTAIL
0.9″   w. 3.8″

SWALLOWTAILS   Here are our largest and most attractive butterflies. Over 20 species occur in the United States and many others are found elsewhere, making the swallowtails a group that is widely known, admired, collected, and studied. Closely related to the swallowtails are the parnassians, more common in the West. These lack the "tail" on the hindwings that gives the swallowtails their name. The caterpillars pupate on the ground. The mountain butterfly is an example of this group.

Swallowtails are predominantly black or yellow. Some species occur in several forms. Female tiger swallowtails may be either yellow or black, the black form being more common in the South. Eggs are smooth, round, and flattened at the base. The caterpillars are generally smooth, lacking spines, though pipevine swallowtails have several rows of fleshy horns, or tubercles (p. 81). Larvae have a collapsible organ behind the head which emits a musky odor that protects them from some predators. The green or brown chrysalis rests on its end, supported by a loop of silk at the middle.

The swallowtails illustrated here are easy to identify in spite of variations in color. Their caterpillars and food plants are shown on the next page. The zebra swallowtail has the longest tail of any native species. The giant swallowtail is the largest, with a spread of 4 to 5½ inches. It is most common in the Southeast. Its larvae are occasionally destructive to citrus orchards. Both male and female black swallowtails have a double row of yellow spots, but those of the female are smaller. Yellow spots on the forewings and greenish hindwings mark the spicebush swallowtail. The pipevine lacks the yellow spots.

SPICEBUSH on sassafras

ZEBRA on pawpaw

PIPEVINE on pipevine

BLACK on parsley

GIANT on orange

TIGER on wild cherry

SWALLOWTAIL CATERPILLARS
and their food plants

82

ARCTIC SKIPPER
0.3" w. 0.9"

SILVER-SPOTTED SKIPPER
(underside)
0.7" w. 1.9"
with larva
on black
locust

SOUTHERN
CLOUDY WING
0.6" w. 1.5"

SKIPPERS About 200 kinds of skippers are native, and this is only one-tenth of the total number. Their rapid, darting flight gives them their name. These small butterflies have characteristics of moths. Some rest with the hindwings or both wings horizontal as moths do. The smooth caterpillars have large heads and thin "necks." They feed on locust, clover, sedges, and other plants. The silver-spotted skipper is the most common of the large skippers. Many are much smaller than this.

Silver-spotted Skipper

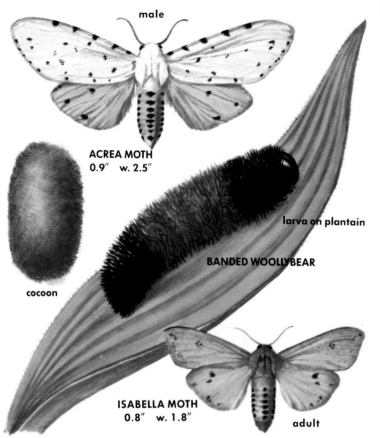

male

ACREA MOTH
0.9″ w. 2.5″

larva on plantain

BANDED WOOLLYBEAR

cocoon

ISABELLA MOTH
0.8″ w. 1.8″

adult

ACREA AND ISABELLA MOTHS represent a family of some 200 American species. Acrea is one of the most common eastern moths, easily identified by its spotted abdomen. The female's hindwings are white. Caterpillars feed on many plants, including garden species. Banded woollybear, the well-known Isabella moth caterpillar, is abundant in the autumn, feeding on asters, sunflowers, clover, and other plants. The larvae of both species mix body hair with silk in making their cocoons.

Acrea Moth and
Banded Woollybear

84

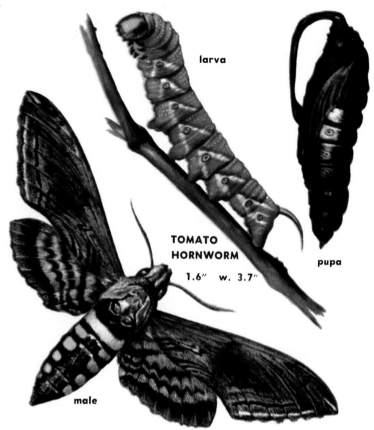

larva

pupa

**TOMATO
HORNWORM**

1.6″ w. 3.7″

male

SPHINX MOTHS Some 100 species of these thick-
bodied, narrow-winged moths live in this country. Their
common names, as tomato worm and tobacco worm,
indicate the food plants sought by the larvae of a few
species. Leaves, and sometimes fruits, are eaten. Some
species feed on potatoes; others eat birch, willow, ca-
talpa, grape, and other plants, occasionally damaging
nurseries and vineyards. The larvae are large and usually have a tail or horn. Some rear back into a belliger-
ent attitude when molested, but none are poisonous, as
is sometimes believed. Braconid wasps lay their eggs in

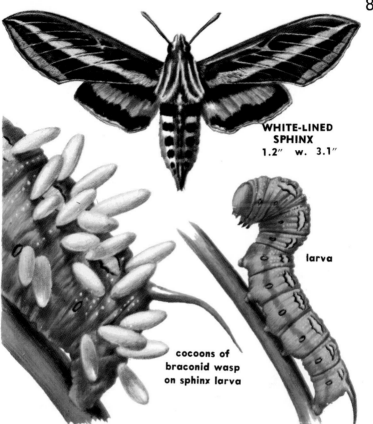

WHITE-LINED SPHINX
1.2" w. 3.1"

larva

cocoons of
braconid wasp
on sphinx larva

the living caterpillars, which the wasp larvae eat. Caterpillars of Sphinx moths covered with wasp cocoons are often seen. Caterpillars pupate in the ground, and some may be recognized by the free tongue case, which forms a loop at one end. The adults of common species are identified by abdominal or wing markings. The sucking-tube mouth is long, enabling Sphinx moths to get nectar and pollinate tubular flowers, such as nicotina, petunia, honeysuckle, trumpet vine, and many others.

Tomato Hornworm
and White-lined Sphinx

86

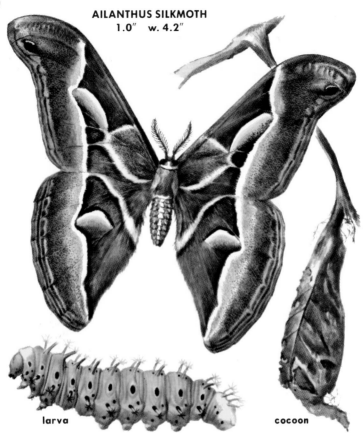

AILANTHUS SILKMOTH
1.0″   w. 4.2″

larva   cocoon

AILANTHUS SILKMOTH   This moth was imported from China, where a coarse grade of silk is obtained from its cocoons. Since 1861, it has become firmly established in the East. The silk industry, which it was hoped this moth would start, never materialized. The large caterpillars are controlled by natural enemies, and since they feed chiefly on ailanthus, a weed tree, they are not harmful. These are our only large moths with white tufts on the abdomen.

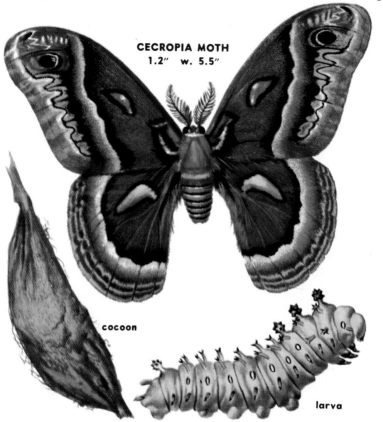

CECROPIA MOTH
1.2″   w. 5.5″

cocoon

larva

CECROPIA MOTH The large, tubercle-studded cecropia larvae feed on cherry, maple, willow, and many other plants. The large, tough, brown cocoons are firmly attached to branches and are easily found in winter. Outdoors, the huge moths emerge in late spring or summer, but when cocoons are brought indoors they hatch earlier. The emergence of the adult is a sight to see. The wrinkled, velvety wings unfold till they are 5 or 6 inches across—something worth watching!

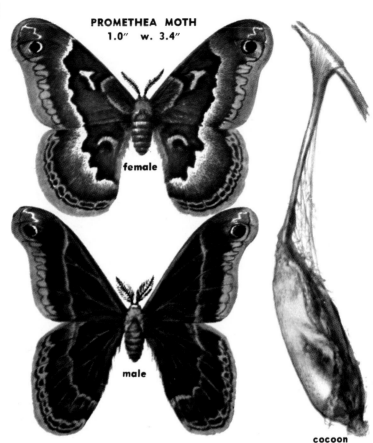

PROMETHEA MOTH
1.0" w. 3.4"

female

male

cocoon

PROMETHEA MOTH This moth, sometimes called the spicebush silkmoth, has a bluish-green larva with two pairs of short red horns near the head. It feeds on many plants, including sassafras, wild cherry, tulip tree, sweet gum, and spicebush. Collect the compact cocoons, each wrapped in a dry leaf, and watch the adults emerge in spring. Recognize the male by its darker maroon color. The female is a bit larger, lighter, and browner, with slightly different markings.

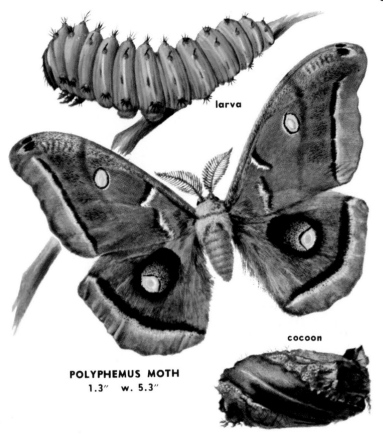

larva

cocoon

POLYPHEMUS MOTH
1.3″ w. 5.3″

POLYPHEMUS MOTH Because of its gigantic size and the "eye-spots" on the wings, this night-flying silk moth was named after the one-eyed giant, Polyphemus, of Greek mythology. The green larvae, sometimes over 3 inches long, feed on oak, hickory, elm, maple, birch, and other trees and shrubs. They spin their plump cocoons either on the ground or attached to a twig. These moths are more common in the South, where there are two broods a year.

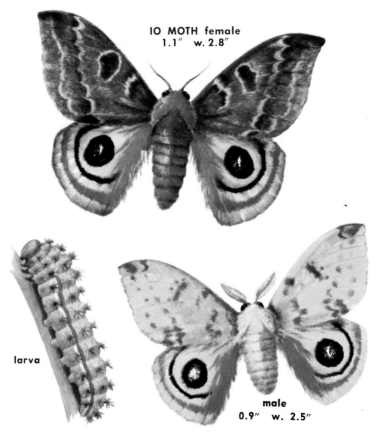

IO MOTH female
1.1″ w. 2.8″

larva

male
0.9″ w. 2.5″

IO MOTHS Three very similar species are found in this country. The larvae are of particular interest, for their sharp spines are mildly poisonous. Recognize them by their horizontal red-and-white stripe. Handle them with care when you find them—on corn and other garden and many wild plants. Ichneumon flies (p. 137) often attack the larvae. The cocoon is found on the ground in dead leaves. The adult male is smaller than the female and has bright yellow forewings.

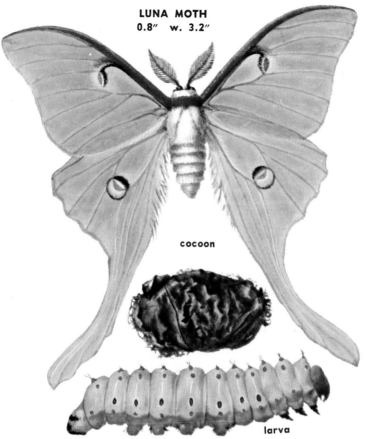

LUNA MOTH
0.8″ w. 3.2″

cocoon

larva

LUNA MOTH This handsome moth, with its striking long tails and delicate green color, makes a lasting impression on those who see it for the first time. It is a favorite with collectors. The larvae, smaller than other night-fliers, feed on many trees, including sweet gum, walnut, hickory, and persimmon. The cocoons are usually spun on the ground. Adults are similar in appearance; some have more purple on the borders of the wings than others.

ULTRONIA
UNDERWING

larva

with wings shut

CLOUDED LOCUST UNDERWING 0.8″ w. 2.4″

UNDERWING MOTHS There are over 100 species of these attractive moths in the United States, and a variety of underwings can be found in every locality. Collect them in woods at night after painting tree trunks and stumps with a mixture of brown sugar and fermented fruit juice as bait. When the adult rests on bark with its wings folded, it can scarcely be seen. In flight, the bright colors of the underwings are in sharp contrast to the drab pattern of the forewings.

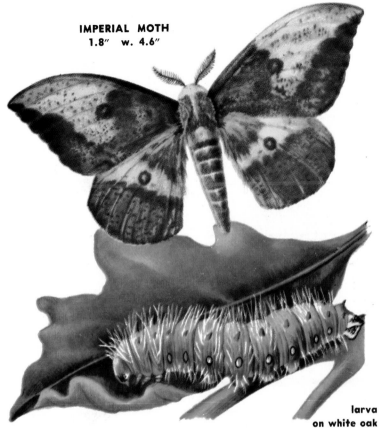

IMPERIAL MOTH
1.8" w. 4.6"

larva
on white oak

IMPERIAL AND REGAL MOTHS These moths are closely related to the large silk moths. The hairy imperial caterpillar, with short horns near the head, varies from green to brown. It feeds on pine, hickory, oak, maple, and other trees. No cocoon is formed, the pupa resting in the ground. The forewings of the male are purplish; those of the female are richer in yellows. The larvae of regal moths, which feed on walnuts, have large, red, curved horns.

Imperial

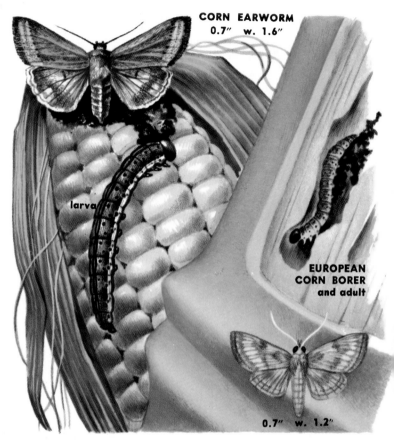

CORN EARWORM
0.7" w. 1.6"

larva

EUROPEAN
CORN BORER
and adult

0.7" w. 1.2"

CORN EARWORM AND BORERS Everyone who has husked sweet corn has seen the greenish or brown larva of the corn earworm, found almost everywhere. It feeds on other garden crops, too, and pupates underground. The European corn borer became established near Boston in 1917 and has spread widely since, doing millions of dollars' damage to corn. The larvae bore into stalks, weakening and breaking them. Control is difficult, as borers live in wild plants also.

European
Corn Borer

Corn Earworm

WHITE-MARKED TUSSOCK MOTH
and larva on maple

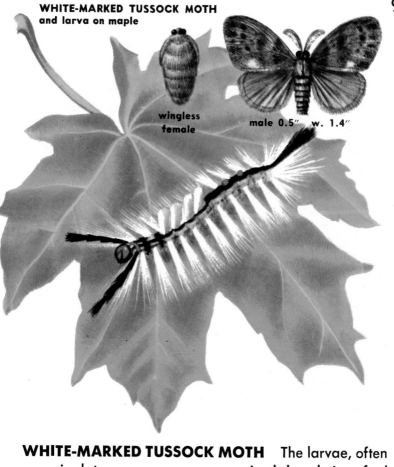

wingless female

male 0.5″ w. 1.4″

WHITE-MARKED TUSSOCK MOTH   The larvae, often seen in late summer, are recognized by their tufted white hairs and attractive contrasting colors. They are pests of most shade and ornamental trees and are best controlled by destroying cocoons in winter. The egg masses are laid by the wingless females on the surface of their cocoons. Eggs hatch in spring, but the larvae are not noticeable till summer. Adults are small and inconspicuous.

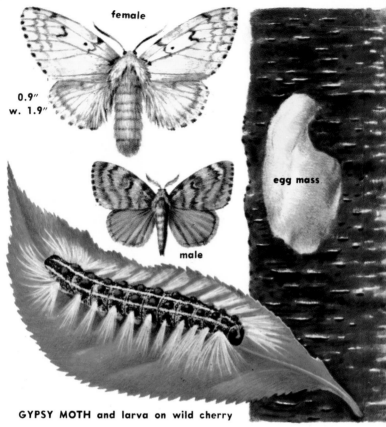

female

0.9"
w. 1.9"

egg mass

male

GYPSY MOTH and larva on wild cherry

GYPSY MOTH   The gypsy and the brown-tail moth are
European relatives of the white-marked tussock moth
which, unfortunately, have become established in this
country. The larvae, somewhat similar to tussock moths,
without tussocks, eat the leaves of most shade and forest
trees. They tend to feed at night. Larvae pupate in midsummer and adults emerge shortly.
The female flies but little. She lays a
mass of eggs, covering them with
hair and scales. These hatch in spring.

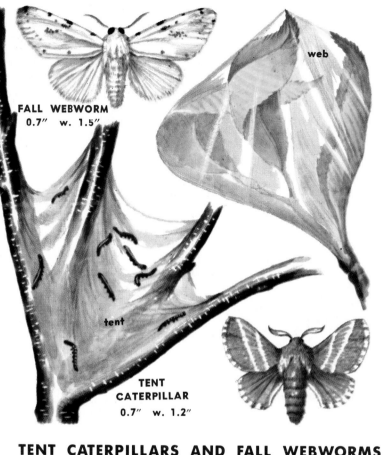

FALL WEBWORM
0.7" w. 1.5"

web

tent

TENT
CATERPILLAR
0.7" w. 1.2"

TENT CATERPILLARS AND FALL WEBWORMS

These pests of many forest, shade, and ornamental trees are not closely related, but are often confused. Both build webs, but that of the fall webworm covers the leaves. The tent caterpillar web, built only in spring, is at the crotch of branches. Adult webworms, with variable black spots on forewings, lay eggs on leaves. Tent caterpillar egg masses are found on twigs in winter. Remove them to control this insect.

Tent Caterpillar
and Fall Webworm

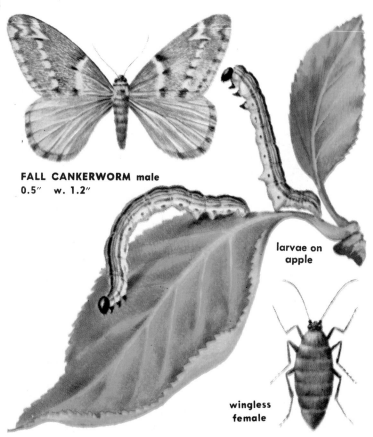

FALL CANKERWORM male
0.5″   w. 1.2″

larvae on
apple

wingless
female

CANKERWORMS These pests of apple, other fruit, and shade trees are worth watching as they lope along on their true and false legs. Sometimes they spin a silken thread and hang suspended in mid-air. Fall and spring cankerworms are equally obnoxious. The wingless females lay their eggs on bark. After feasting on leaves, the larvae pupate underground. The adults emerge late in fall and can be trapped by bands of sticky paper around tree trunks.

Fall Cankerworm

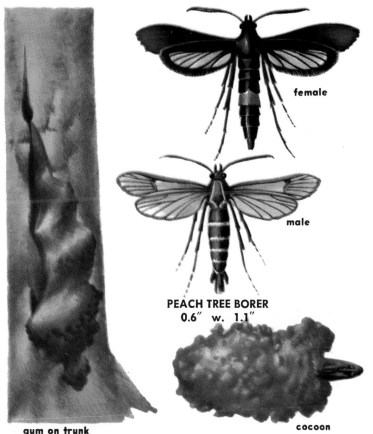

female

male

PEACH TREE BORER
0.6″ w. 1.1″

gum on trunk

cocoon

PEACH TREE BORER larvae enter the tree as soon as they hatch from the eggs, which have been laid on the bark. The larvae burrows can be regonized by exuding gum on the surface. After spending the winter as a larva, the borer pupates in a crude cocoon. The adult emerges in about a month and mates. The female lays a new mass of several hundred eggs. This pest is a native insect which is believed to have fed on wild plum and cherry before peaches were introduced.

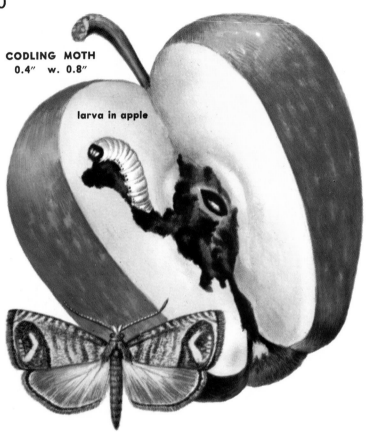

CODLING MOTH
0.4" w. 0.8"

larva in apple

CODLING MOTH This pest, introduced from Europe, is now widely distributed. Tiny eggs are deposited on leaves. As they hatch, the larvae enter the new fruit. Later, larvae hatch from eggs laid on the apples. Also on cherry, peach, pear, and walnut. After feeding in the fruit, larvae pupate on the bark. There are often several generations a year. Late larvae hibernate in winter and pupate the following spring after additional feeding.

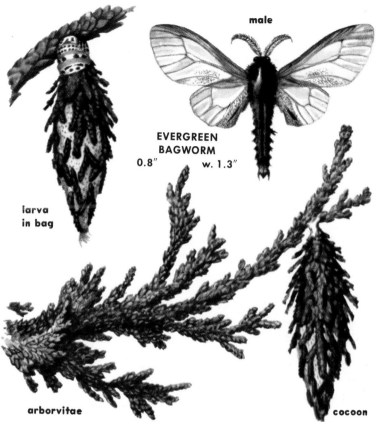

male

**EVERGREEN
BAGWORM**
0.8"   w. 1.3"

larva
in bag

arborvitae

cocoon

BAGWORMS occasionally become pests locally. Their life history is strange. The wingless and legless female, after mating, crawls back into her "bag" and lays hundreds of yellow eggs, which hatch in spring. The young larvae feed on leaves of many kinds of trees, building their conical bags as they feed. Later they bind their bags to twigs and pupate. The male emerges, seeks a female, and mates. Several related moths make bags that are similar in design.

Evergreen
Bagworm

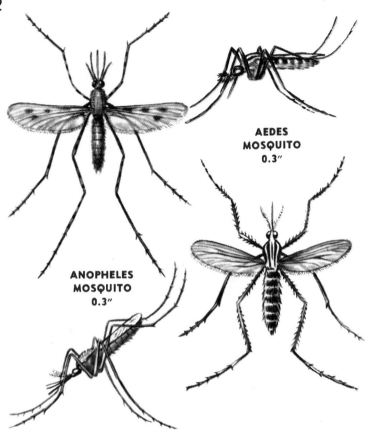

AEDES
MOSQUITO
0.3"

ANOPHELES
MOSQUITO
0.3"

MOSQUITOES This large group of small but important insects has been amply studied as part of public-health campaigns against malaria and yellow fever. The conquest of malaria is a scientific milestone. The common carriers of the disease, the anopheles mosquitoes, are recognized by the "three-pronged" beak of the female and by the tilted position they assume when resting. The aedes mosquitoes, one of which carries yellow fever, are more like the common house and swamp mosquito in appearance. The disease carrier is limited to tropics and

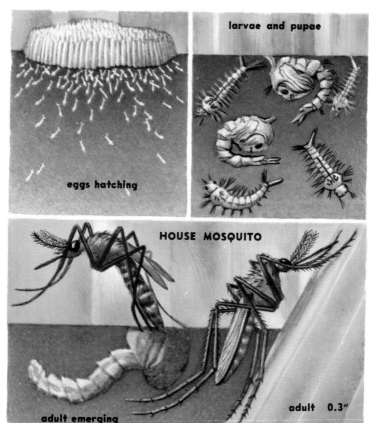

larvae and pupae

eggs hatching

HOUSE MOSQUITO

adult emerging

adult 0.3"

subtropics. Female culex mosquitoes lay rafts of several hundred eggs, which hatch in a few days into larval wrigglers. In a week or so these pupate, and the adults soon emerge. Male mosquitoes feed on nectar. Females bite to feed on blood and hence can transmit disease. Mosquitoes have been controlled by draining swamps and by the wide use of insecticides. The long-range dangers in these methods needs further study. Both as adults and larvae, mosquitoes are important food for animals such as fish, birds, and dragonflies.

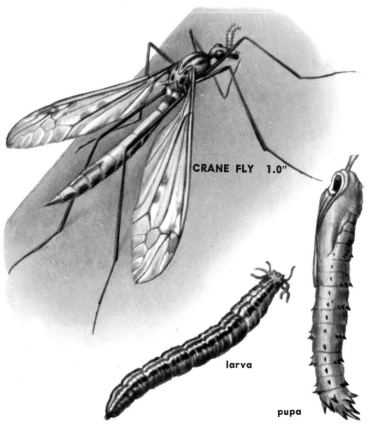

CRANE FLY 1.0"

larva

pupa

CRANE FLIES Adult crane flies are sometimes mistaken for giant mosquitoes. But the adults, often seen around electric lights, may not eat at all. Some are apparently predaceous. The female lays several hundred eggs on damp soil. The larvae burrow into the ground or decaying wood. Only a few attack plants. In a few weeks they pupate, and in about a week appear as adults. Crane flies form a large group, with nearly 1,500 species in this country.

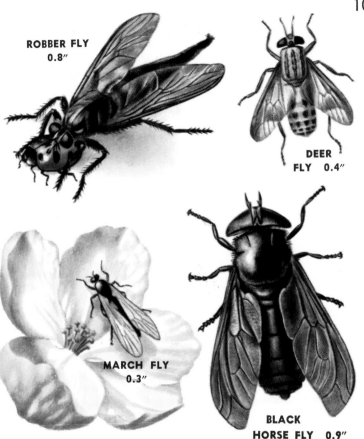

ROBBER FLY
0.8"

DEER
FLY 0.4"

MARCH FLY
0.3"

BLACK
HORSE FLY 0.9"

FLIES include serious pests of plants and animals which cause losses running into millions. The vast majority are harmless; many are beneficial as pollinators, parasites of pests, and food for other animals. The robber fly preys on many insects, some larger than itself. The deer fly and the black fly can make a camper miserable. March flies (which are more common late in spring) are often seen on flowers. The black horse fly, sometimes a full inch long, bites severely. Some flies transmit disease as they bite infected animals and then others.

BLUEBOTTLE FLY 0.5"

larva

GREENBOTTLE FLY
0.5"

pupa

BLUEBOTTLE AND GREENBOTTLE FLIES are attractive insects whose larvae (maggots) break down and recycle decaying or dead organic matter. Eggs are laid on dead animals, garbage, sewage, or in open wounds of animals. Some related species parasitize and kill animals and even man. Eggs hatch very soon after being laid; the larvae are mature in less than 2 weeks. The short life cycle means there are several generations a season.

Bluebottle
and Greenbottle

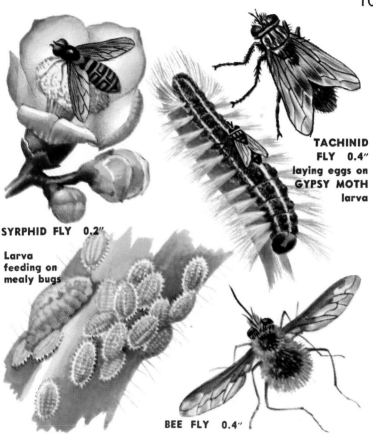

SYRPHID FLY 0.2"

Larva
feeding on
mealy bugs

TACHINID
FLY 0.4"
laying eggs on
GYPSY MOTH
larva

BEE FLY 0.4"

TACHINID AND OTHER FLIES Tachinid flies are beneficial insects which help control injurious ones. More than 1,400 species have been described. Because these flies are prolific, their value as parasites is increased. Syrphid flies, known as flower or drone flies, are similar insects. They are often seen approching a flower, coming to an abrupt stop and hovering in mid-air. The larvae eat aphids and scales. The fuzzy, squat bee fly lives in nests of bees, and its larvae often attack and feed on larvae of bees and other insects.

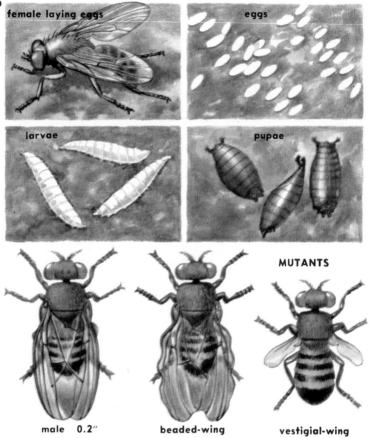

female laying eggs

eggs

larvae

pupae

MUTANTS

male 0.2"   beaded-wing   vestigial-wing

FRUIT FLIES These small and rather important flies (several hundred species) are often seen around rotting or fermenting fruit and fungi. Their claim to fame rests on scientific uses to which they have been put. One species, in particular, has been used in studies of inheritance. The fact that their life cycle is less than 2 weeks enhances their value in this work. They are easily grown in the laboratory, where interesting forms have appeared naturally or from exposure to experimental radiation.

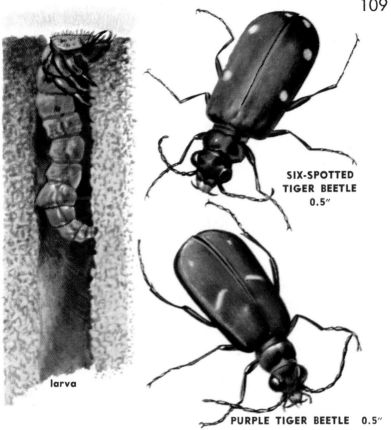

SIX-SPOTTED
TIGER BEETLE
0.5″

PURPLE TIGER BEETLE   0.5″

larva

TIGER BEETLES These handsome beetles are often seen on summer afternoons darting in and out of paths. They are widely distributed and quite common, but agile, swift, and difficult to catch. Eggs are laid in the soil. The flat-headed, hump-backed, predatory larvae dig deep burrows and wait at the openings to catch passing insects in their powerful jaws. Some tiger beetles living on beaches or other sandy areas are protectively colored gray.

Six-spotted

110

ROSE CHAFER 0.4"

ROSE CHAFER This slim, hairy beetle is one of the many scarab beetles, a large family of over 30,000 species, diverse in size and appearance. Some are important pests. The rose chafer feeds on roses, grapes, and a variety of other plants. Adults appear in late spring and early summer, eating both leaves and flowers. The larvae burrow into the ground, where they feed on roots, especially those of grasses. Control of the rose chafer is difficult.

Rose Chafer

Related forms

JAPANESE BEETLE 0.4"

JAPANESE BEETLE When these Japanese insects were first discovered on plants in New Jersey in 1916, experts could scarcely find a dozen. Now thousands can be collected daily, and control is a serious problem. The small, white grubs feed on the roots of grasses, damaging lawns. The larvae dig deep for winter and pupate the following spring. The adults emerge in midsummer and feed on cultivated plants and fruits. After mating, eggs are deposited in soil.

112

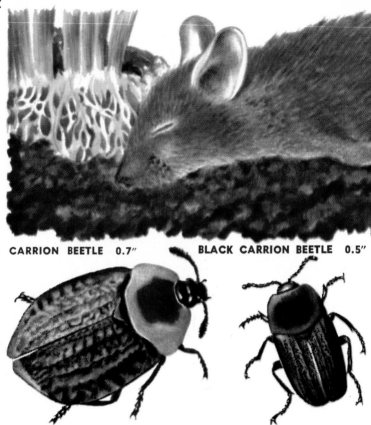

CARRION BEETLE 0.7" **BLACK CARRION BEETLE 0.5"**

CARRION BEETLES form a family of over 100 species, in two groups: the carrion and the burying beetles. The former are smaller, flattened insects which, as scavengers, feed on decaying animal matter. Some kinds are predators, feeding on worms and insects; a few eat plants. Both larvae and adults have similar feeding habits. It is

reported that the larger burying beetles, which are sometimes brightly colored, dig under the carcass of a small animal till it falls into the hole

AMERICAN BURYING BEETLES 1.2"

HAIRY BURYING BEETLE 0.7"   HAIRY ROVE BEETLE 0.8"

and is actually buried to serve as food for the larvae. The eggs are deposited on the corpse. The larvae of some species develop rapidly, reaching maturity in about a week. Rove beetles, of another family, are also scavengers or predators, have short wing-covers and superficially resemble the earwigs (p. 29). They are a larger group—over 3,000 species are reported for this country. Some live in fungi or in ants' nests. Some squirt a malodorous mist at enemies.

Hairy Rove Beetle and Carrion Beetles

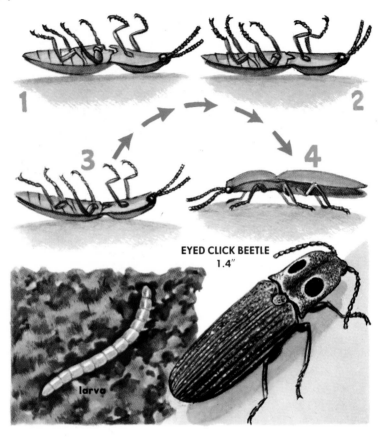

EYED CLICK BEETLE
1.4"

larva

CLICK BEETLES form a family of some 500 American species. The eyed click beetle is a striking example. If it falls or lands on its back, it lies quietly for perhaps a minute. Then, with a loud click, it flips into the air. If it is lucky, it lands on its feet and runs away; otherwise it tries again. The larvae of click beetles, known as wireworms, live in the ground or in rotten wood. Many click beetle larvae feed on roots, sometimes injuring potatoes and other crops. Some eat other insects.

Click Beetles

Eyed Click

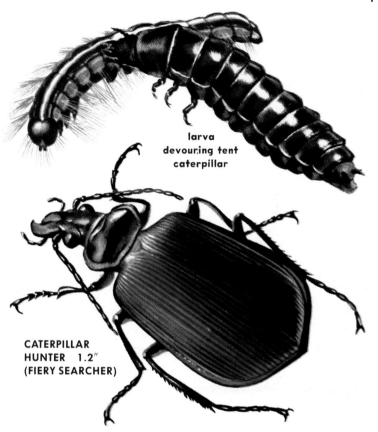

larva
devouring tent
caterpillar

CATERPILLAR
HUNTER 1.2"
(FIERY SEARCHER)

CATERPILLAR HUNTERS are a group of fairly large and very attractive beetles. The family to which they belong, the ground beetles, is also large (some 2,000 American species) and is closely related to the tiger beetles (p. 109). Most are predaceous, feeding on insects and other small animals. Larvae of the caterpillar hunters attack and feed on caterpillars of gypsy moths, tent caterpillars, and others. Some adults squirt an acrid fluid at predators or on unwary collectors.

FIREFLIES 0.5"

FIREFLIES AND GLOWWORMS are not flies at all, but soft-bodied beetles belonging to two families; they are most unusual insects. About 130 species are known in this country, and many more, even more marvelous, are found in the tropics. The light-giving property, or luminescence, is not confined to adults. In one family, the glowworms, the eggs and larvae glow also. Females of some species are short-winged or wingless. Fireflies are of little economic importance. They add to the pleasure of a summer night. Thousands of these insects flashing in unison is a breathtaking sight. Fireflies have posed a problem scientists have not yet completely solved—that of "cold" light. Study of this phenomenon may have

larva

female

wide practical applications. In the species shown, it is the last segment of the abdomen which contains the light-producing tissue. This is very fatty and includes a net-work of nerves and airtubes. Through the latter, oxygen for the light-producing process is obtained. In ordinary rapid oxidation much more heat than light is produced; here, heat production is negligible.

The larvae live underground or in rotted wood or rubbish, feeding on worms and snails. The adults are also largely predaceous, but some of the common fireflies may not feed at all in the adult stage. Put some in a jar and watch the action.

Glowworm

Other Fireflies

NINE-SPOTTED LADYBIRD 0.3"

aphids

CONVERGENT LADYBIRD

larva

LADYBIRD BEETLES are probably the best known and most valued of our beetles. We have some 350 species in this country, though the family is world-wide in distribution. Lutz says the name can be traced back to the Middle Ages, when these beetles were dedicated to the Virgin—hence the name ladybird or ladybug. Both larvae and adults of many species feed on aphids. In California, where these pests and scale insects cause serious damage to citrus trees, native and imported ladybird beetles have been successfully used to hold the pests in check. When the cottony-cushion scale from Australia (pp. 40-41) began to spread through California orange groves, the entire industry was threatened. An Australian ladybug

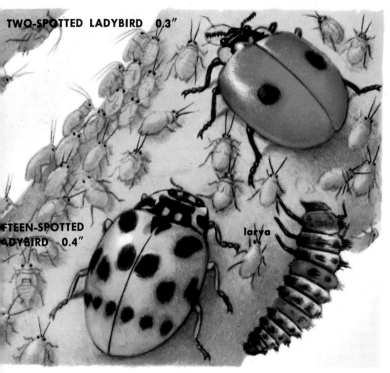

TWO-SPOTTED LADYBIRD   0.3"

FTEEN-SPOTTED
ADYBIRD   0.4"

larva

which feeds entirely on the scale was imported and within
a few years the scale was under control. About 3,000
beetles will protect an acre of trees. The common species
are generally similar in appearance but differ in the number of spots. All have very short legs, which distinguish
these beetles from other garden beetles (pp. 120-125).
Ladybird beetles lay their eggs on plants infected with
aphids or scales. The larvae feed on the aphids and pass
through four growth stages. When mature, they pupate in
the remains of the last larval skin.
Adults assemble by the thousands before cold weather sets in and hibernate under fallen branches or rocks.

Other
Ladybirds   15-spotted
Ladybird

GARDEN BEETLES

Garden beetles are pests of the garden as well as the farm. Other beetles are destructive in the garden also, such as the Japanese beetle, and several weevils. Crops and garden plants often have weakened natural defenses against insects such as beetles as a result of selective breeding, making these plants ideal targets for attack. Growing lots of the same crop plant in one area, as we do in traditional farming, enhances the chance for severe infestations from pest species. Wild relatives of crops and garden plants are more resistant to insect attack.

MEXICAN BEAN BEETLE is related to the common ladybird, and is one of the fairly large group within the ladybird family that feed on plants. Eggs are laid on the undersides of leaves. Spiny, yellow larvae eat the soft leaf tissue, leaving the veins behind. They eat pods too, stripping a plant in short order. Adults have similar feeding habits. Bean beetles feed on members of the pea family, wild and cultivated—peas, beans, alfalfa, and soybeans.

COLORADO POTATO BEETLE is an example of how a relatively unimportant insect can change its role as the environment changes. This beetle was once native to the Rockies, living on nightshade and other wild members of the potato family. When settlers began to grow potatoes, this new food gave the beetles a fresh start. They prospered and spread throughout practically all of the U.S. Eggs are laid in clusters on the leaves, which both larvae and adults eat. Larvae pupate in the ground.

STRIPED BLISTER BEETLE or striped potato beetle has interesting relatives that parasitize bees. This species has a complex life history with unusual larvae. It feeds on potatoes, tomatoes, and related plants. Other species feed on goldenrod, alfalfa, clover, and other wild plants.

MEXICAN BEAN BEETLE
0.3"
eggs and larva

122

COLORADO POTATO BEETLE

larva

adult
0.4"

eggs

STRIPED BLISTER BEETLE 0.7"

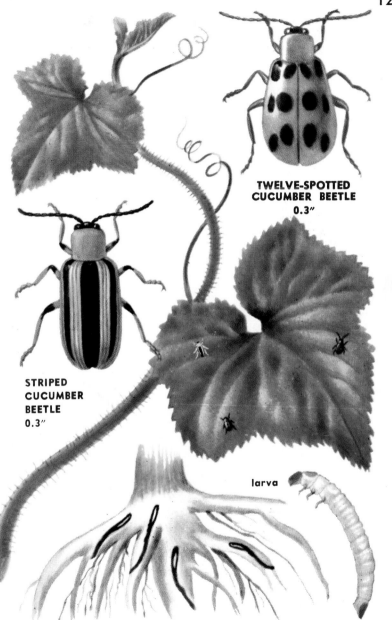

**TWELVE-SPOTTED
CUCUMBER BEETLE
0.3"**

**STRIPED
CUCUMBER
BEETLE
0.3"**

larva

larva in roots of corn

CUCUMBER BEETLES   The striped and spotted cucumber beetles are common garden pests. The larvae of the former attack roots, and the adults eat leaves of cucumber, squash, and related plants. The 12-spotted cucumber beetle is an even worse pest, feeding on many other plants besides those of the squash family. It appears early in the season and stays late. In the South, the larvae attack the roots of corn, oats, and other grasses.

ASPARAGUS BEETLES, two species of them, ravage the asparagus crop. Adults hibernate in the ground, emerging in spring to feed on young shoots. Eggs are soon laid and larvae attack shoots, "leaves," and fruit, stripping the plant. The life cycle takes only about a month, so there are several broods a year. Both species, the common asparagus beetle and the spotted asparagus beetle, were introduced from Europe, one about 90, and the other about 70, years ago.

CONTROL OF GARDEN PESTS   Control of garden insects first requires a knowledge of which pests are involved and something of their eating habits. Not every insect you find on plants in your garden is a pest. Many are beneficial. It is important, therefore, to identify the insect. If you cannot, seek aid of your county agent, college of agriculture, museum, or the U.S. Department of Agriculture (see p. 9). Once you know the insect, proper control measures can be learned from the same sources. State and Federal agricultural agencies have pamphlets on control of garden pests. The pamphlets are available (usually free or at a nominal cost) upon request. Methods of pest control are being constantly changed to meet new conditions.

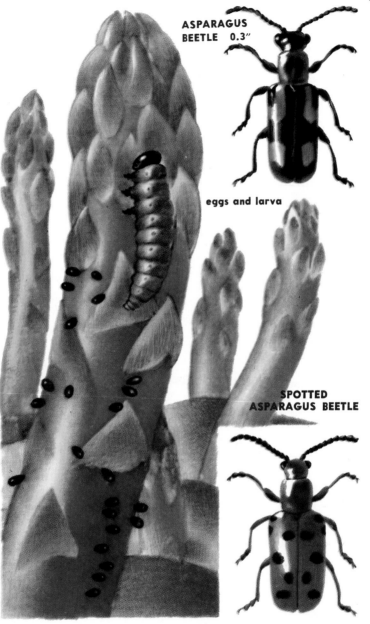

ASPARAGUS BEETLE 0.3"

eggs and larva

SPOTTED ASPARAGUS BEETLE

WHIRLIGIG BEETLES   0.6"

DIVING BEETLE   1.1"

MAYFLY larva

DIVING BEETLE larva

WATER BEETLES are not to be confused with water bugs (pp. 48-49), though they are often found in the same habitat. Whirligig beetles, true to their name, whirl or swim at the surface. They dive when disturbed and are good fliers also. Eggs are laid on water plants; larvae feed on water animals. Eggs of diving beetles are deposited in the tissues of water plants. They hatch into larvae commonly known as water tigers, which attack water insects, small fish, tadpoles, even one another. After a month or so, larvae leave the water and pupate in the ground. Adults are active all year. Their method

WATER SCAVENGER 1.3"

of carrying a bubble of air down with them at the tip of their abdomen is interesting to watch.

Water scavengers (225 species) include our largest water beetles, some over 3 inches long. Eggs are laid in a silken wrapping, attached to a floating leaf. The predaceous larvae feed like those of diving beetles. Pupae form in soil by late summer, and emerge in about 2 weeks. Adults also are active in all seasons. They carry air as a film on the underside of the body. These and other water insects can be kept in an aquarium and fed bits of meat.

128

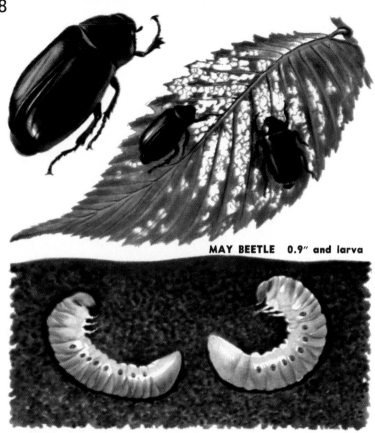

MAY BEETLE 0.9" and larva

MAY BEETLES or June bugs form a group of over 100 American species, widely distributed and difficult to control. White eggs are laid in an earth-covered ball amid roots on which the white grubs feed for 2 or 3 years. These pupate underground in fall, and adults appear the following spring. Adults feed on leaves of many common trees. They are attracted to electric lights. Birds and small mammals, such as skunks and even pigs, root out grubs and eat them.

GREEN JUNE BEETLE 0.9" and larva

GREEN JUNE BEETLE Often called the figeater, this beetle feeds on many plants, eating roots, stems, and leaves. Larvae are found in soil or manure. They move by bristles on their backs instead of by their short legs. Adults fly in large numbers, making a loud buzzing which is somewhat similar to the buzzing of bumblebees. These insects are more common in the South, where the adults damage apricots, figs, grapes, melons, and other fleshy fruits.

130

female

DUNG
BEETLES
0.8"

male

RHINOCEROS BEETLE
1.0"

TUMBLEBUGS 0.8"

SCARAB BEETLES, including the rose chafer, Japanese beetle, and May beetle, form a large family totalling more than 30,000 species, of which well over 1,300 are found in this country. Many are scavengers, adapted for living in or on the ground. Larvae are usually large white grubs found in the soil. Of the many scarabs, the dung beetles and tumblebugs are outstanding. These are the beetles held sacred by the Egyptians. The adults form balls of dung and roll them about giving the impression

EASTERN HERCULES BEETLE
female

OX BEETLE 1.0"

EASTERN HERCULES BEETLE
male 2-2.5"

of being industrious workers. Eggs are laid in the ball, which is buried. The ferocious-looking rhinoceros beetles and their relatives, the ox beetles, are the largest of the scarabs. All are harmless. Some are 2 inches long; much larger tropical forms occur. Males have more prominent horns than females. The larvae are found in rotted wood or rich soil. Collectors prize the adults.

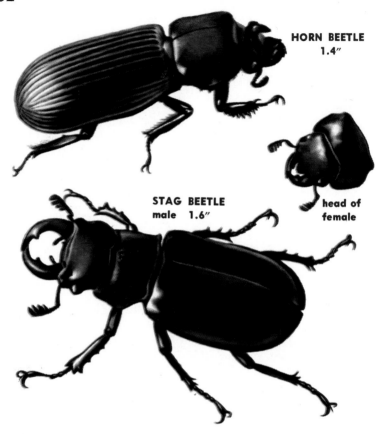

HORN BEETLE
1.4"

STAG BEETLE
male 1.6"

head of
female

STAG AND HORN BEETLES are related to scarabs. The large stags are so named because the huge mandibles of the males resemble the antlers of stags. Mouth-parts of the females are much smaller. Large white grubs are found in rotted wood—more commonly in the South than elsewhere. Horned-beetle larvae and adults are often found in large colonies in burrows in rotted logs. These beetles make noise by rubbing wing-covers or legs. The adults are harmless.

Stag

Stag

Horn

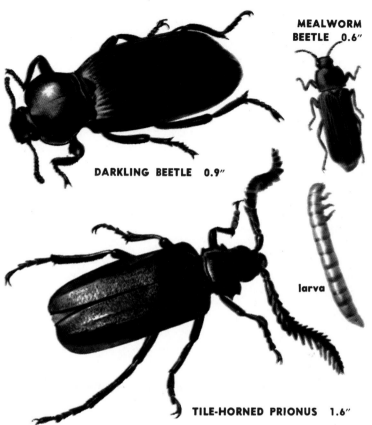

MEALWORM BEETLE 0.6"

DARKLING BEETLE 0.9"

larva

TILE-HORNED PRIONUS 1.6"

DARKLING AND PRIONUS BEETLES   Darkling
beetle larvae are the "mealworms" used for feeding
birds and other small pets. They feed on stored grain
and hence are serious pests. There are about 700 closely
related species. The larvae of prionus beetles are known
as round-headed borers. These attack roots of fruit and
ornamental trees, grape, and other
plants. The antennae, with overlap-
ping plates, slightly longer in the
male, identify the prionus beetles.

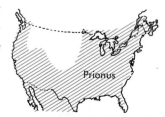

Prionus

ELDER BORER 0.8"

LOCUST BORER 0.7"

PINE SAWYER 1.0" exclusive of antennae

FLATHEADED BORER 0.8"

FLATHEADED AND LONGHORNED BORERS Larvae of many beetles bore into wood, but flatheaded borers (Buprestids), like example above, and longhorned borers (Cerambycids), represented by the locust and elder borers and the pine sawyer, are occasional pests of orchard, shade and forest trees. Larvae of flatheaded borers (at least 500 species in this country) feed mostly just beneath the bark, whereas longhorned borers (over 1,000 species) usually channel far into the trunk or limbs. The attractive locust borer adult is often found on goldenrod.

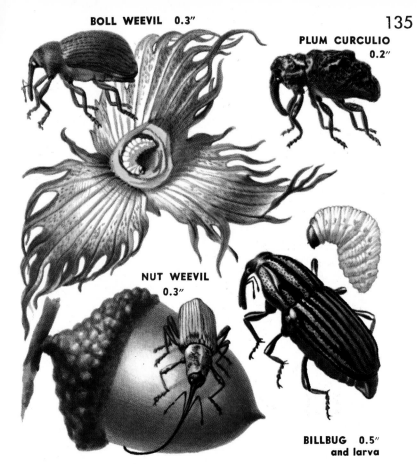

BOLL WEEVIL 0.3"

PLUM CURCULIO 0.2"

NUT WEEVIL 0.3"

BILLBUG 0.5" and larva

WEEVILS are small beetles with mouth-parts modified into a downward-curving beak or snout. The damage done by weevils is estimated at over one billion dollars annually. The grain weevils, important pests of grain, are prolific, with a life cycle of only 4 weeks. Some feed on the roots, others on stored grain. For years, as the boll weevil spread north from Mexico, warnings of the danger to the cotton crop went unheeded. The plum curculio damages peach, cherry, and plum trees. Nut weevils are found in acorns and all other edible nuts.

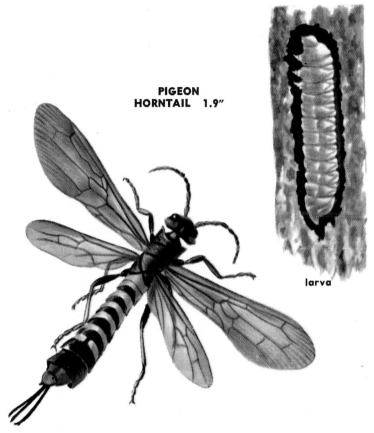

**PIGEON
HORNTAIL 1.9"**

larva

HORNTAILS AND SAWFLIES, closely related, belong
with the bees and wasps but lack the constricted abdomen. Horntails lay their eggs on dead or dying trees.
The larvae are borers, which pupate in their deep tun-
nels. Most sawfly larvae feed on leaves. Horntails are
hosts to the ichneumons (next page), which parasitize the
larvae. The female ichneumon can
locate a horntail burrow under several inches of wood and deposit her
eggs therein.

Horntails and
Sawflies

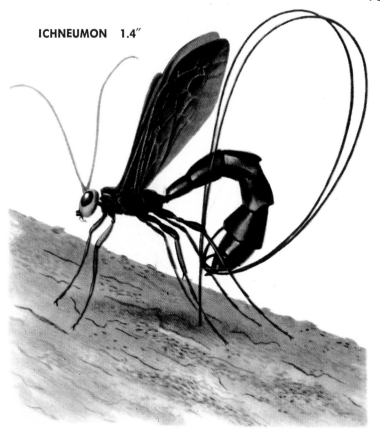

ICHNEUMON 1.4"

ICHNEUMONS, of which there are over 3,000 American species, play an important role in controlling many harmful insects. They belong to the same group of insects as bees and wasps. Their larvae are parasites of caterpillars and of larvae of beetles, flies, and other pests. The long-tailed ichneumon female, with her unusually long ovipositor, attracts attention and is some-times feared by those who do not know she is harmless. This ovipositor can pierce several inches of wood.

Long-tailed Ichneumon

138

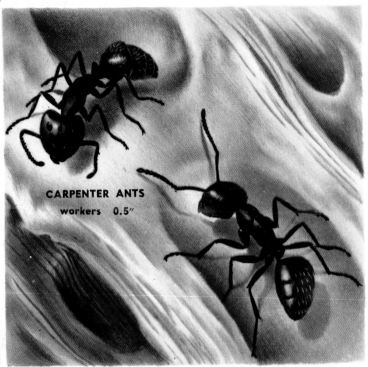

CARPENTER ANTS
workers 0.5"

CARPENTER ANTS Of over 2,500 species of ants known, all are social animals, living and working together in ways that have astonished laymen and naturalists alike. Among the most familiar of insects, they have inspired many a comparison with human society. Carpenter ants and their relatives form one of the largest groups of ants. They build nests and burrows in dead wood, logs, and the timbers of buildings, where they may do considerable damage if allowed to spread. Carpenter ants are found the world over in temperate regions. The workers, which are infertile females, are among the largest known ants.

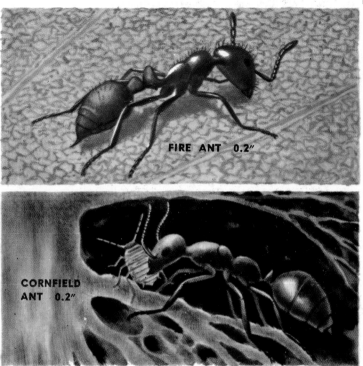

FIRE ANT 0.2"

CORNFIELD ANT 0.2"

FIRE AND CORNFIELD ANTS The fire ants of the Southeast have been known to attack baby birds and sting them to death. Cornfield ants are less ferocious and more interesting. These ants eat the sweet secretions of corn-root aphids. Aphids lay eggs in the ant burrows. When these hatch in spring, the ants place the aphids on knotweed roots till the corn is planted and growing. Then the ants transfer the aphids to the corn roots, thus insuring a constant food supply. Cornfield ants are widely distributed and very abundant. Lutz states that they are the most abundant of all our insects, a fact which makes these small ants important.

Cornfield

Fire

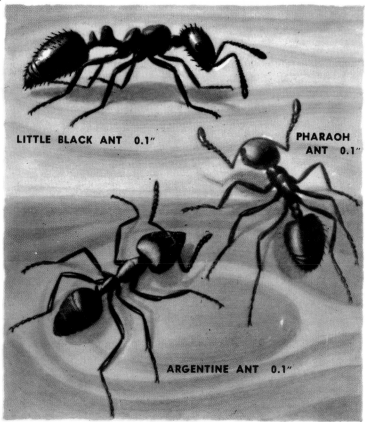

LITTLE BLACK ANT 0.1"

PHARAOH ANT 0.1"

ARGENTINE ANT 0.1"

HOUSEHOLD ANTS Pharaoh ants are small but numerous. They are common invaders of homes, feeding on any sweet foodstuffs. The Argentine ant, native to that country and Brazil, was first found in New Orleans in 1891, and has since become a serious household and garden pest in the South. They may invade nests of other ants and hives of bees. Fortunately they are semitropical and are limited in their movement northward. These ants protect aphids to secure the honey-dew they produce. Little black ants are found outdoors more than within.

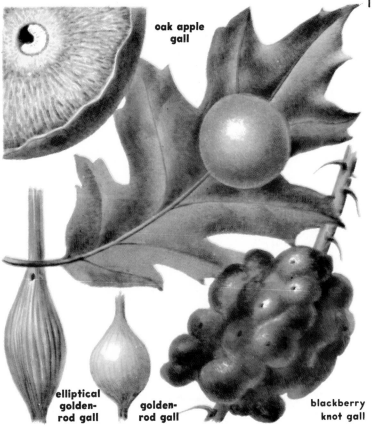

oak apple
gall

elliptical
golden-
rod gall

golden-
rod gall

blackberry
knot gall

INSECT GALLS are not well understood. Small, wasp-like insects (Cynipids), flies, and moths lay eggs in plant tissues. Each insect selects a specific plant. As eggs hatch, the plant tissues around the larvae begin to swell, forming a characteristic gall. The larvae feed on plant juices and pupate in the gall. The adult emerges by burrowing through the side. Some galls are large and woody, some soft, some knobby and spiny. Best-known galls are the oak apples and the galls commonly seen on roses, blackberry, and goldenrods.

142

POTTER WASP
and nest 0.7"

MASON WASP 0.5"   **nest**

MUD WASPS Several families of wasps are represented among those building their nests with mud. Potter
wasps are solitary, each building a vase-shaped nest of
mud on plants. These wasps prey on caterpillars and
beetle larvae. Most mason wasps, in the same family as
the potters, nest in burrows in the soil, but the species
illustrated makes a clay nest on a branch. Best-known
mud wasps are the mud daubers, which make large nests
on walls in attics or deserted buildings. The female builds
the nest of many mud cells. In each she places several

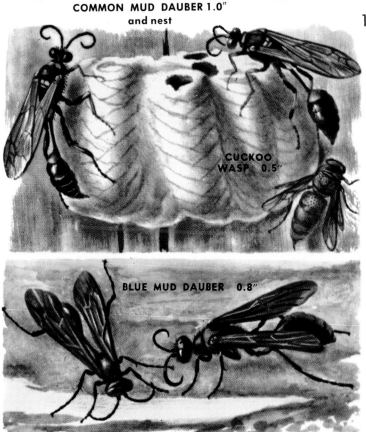

COMMON MUD DAUBER 1.0"
and nest

CUCKOO WASP 0.5"

BLUE MUD DAUBER 0.8"

paralyzed spiders or other insects before she lays the egg and seals the cell. The blue mud dauber uses nests made by the common mud dauber. The female moistens the cell wall, digs through, removes the contents, and refills the cell with her own spiders and egg. The cuckoo wasp, named after the European cuckoo, awaits its opportunity and lays its eggs in the nest of a mud dauber or other wasps while the latter is off searching for a victim. The cuckoo wasp larvae feed on the spiders provided for the young mud dauber.

144

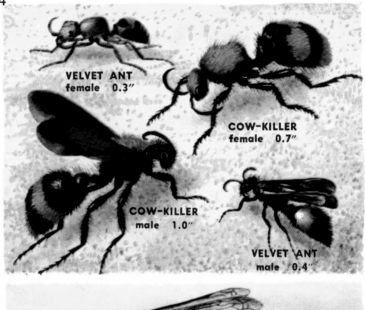

VELVET ANT
female 0.3"

COW-KILLER
female 0.7"

COW-KILLER
male 1.0"

VELVET ANT
male 0.4"

SOLITARY WASP 1.0"

VELVET ANTS   Velvet ants are so named because the wingless females are ant-like. These hairy wasps are parasites of other wasps and bees, especially of the solitary species. The female wasp crawls down the burrow and kills the owner with a powerful sting. She then lays her egg on the owner's larva, which her own larvae later eat. The male wasp does not sting. The solitary, thread-waist wasp illustrated is one of several kinds parasitized by velvet ants.

CICADA KILLER 1.6"

burrow

CICADA KILLER This large solitary wasp digs a burrow a foot or so deep. In side passages the female stores adult cicadas which she has paralyzed by stinging. The heavy cicadas are dragged up a tree by the killer till she can get enough altitude to fly back to her burrow. When the egg hatches, the larva feeds on the helpless cicada. In a week it is full grown and pupates in a loose cocoon. It emerges the following summer, completing its life cycle.

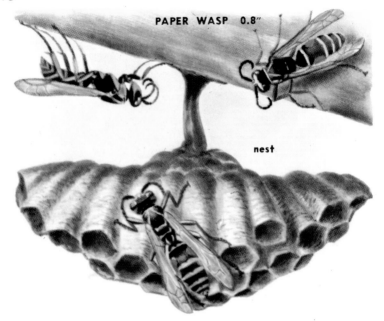

PAPER WASP 0.8"

nest

PAPER WASPS are the common wasps everyone learns to know sooner or later by painful experience. The common paper wasp builds an unprotected paper nest out of wood it chews up. The nest is hung under eaves or in barns, or in other sheltered sites. No food is placed in these nests. After the eggs hatch, the young are fed daily till they pupate. The bald-faced or white-faced hornet builds an oval, covered nest; some nests can accommodate over 10,000 hornets. Unfertilized eggs develop into drones or males. Fertilized eggs grow into workers or queens, depending on the food eaten. Queens make small brood nests in early spring. Yellow jackets, closely related, build nests of varying size, some underground, hidden in rock walls, under logs, and in the walls of buildings. An empty fieldmouse nest is often used.

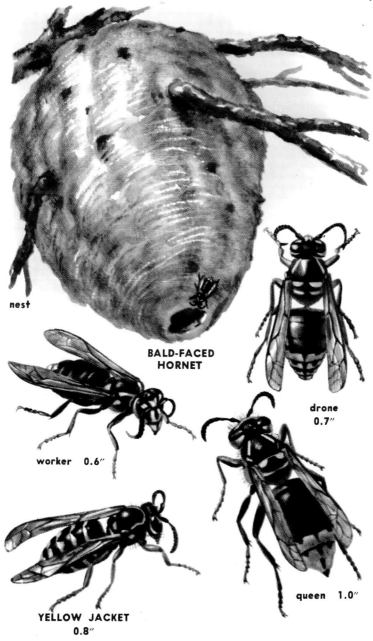

nest

BALD-FACED
HORNET

drone
0.7"

worker 0.6"

queen 1.0"

YELLOW JACKET
0.8"

BUMBLE BEE 1.0"

SWEAT BEE 0.3"

red clover

BEES are distinguished from wasps in a number of minor ways. Their legs have "pollen baskets" of stiff hairs, and the body is hairy also. Bumble bees are larger than most others. Their elongated mouth-parts enable them to pollinate red clover, which no other bee can do. Nests are made underground by the fertile females (queens), which survive the winter. The colony consists of a queen, workers, and drones. Sweat bees, small and brilliantly colored, nest in the ground. They are attracted to perspiration; hence their name. Leafcutting bees are larger and bright-

LEAFCUTTING BEE 0.4″

HONEY BEE 0.5″

FLOWER BEE 0.4″

ly colored also. Their nests, made underground, are lined and divided with leaves which the bees have cut in ovals or circles from roses and other plants. The honey bee is probably the best known of all insects. Honey has been obtained from wild and from kept colonies far back into history. In making honey, bees pollinate fruit trees and other plants. A normal colony of a queen, workers, and drones may contain up to 50,000 bees. Periodically bees swarm, and the old queen goes off to found a new colony, leaving a young queen behind.

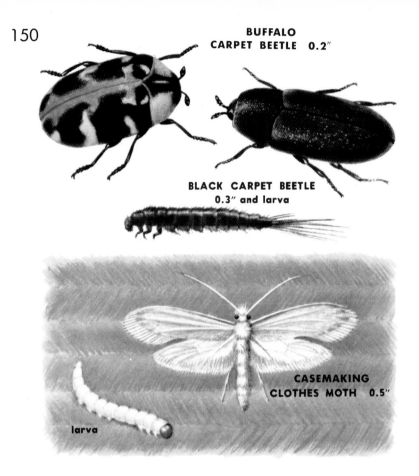

**BUFFALO
CARPET BEETLE 0.2"**

**BLACK CARPET BEETLE
0.3" and larva**

**CASEMAKING
CLOTHES MOTH 0.5"**

larva

PESTS OF CLOTH AND CLOTHING   Carpet beetles
are closely related to other species which destroy specimens in museums. They eat all kinds of animal matter,
thriving on rugs, woolens, fur, leather, hair. The larvae
which do the damage can be controlled by repellents
and poisons. Use these toxic chemicals with caution.
Adult clothes moths do no harm. Females lay white oval
eggs on clothing, leather, etc. These soon hatch into
larvae, which may feed for a year on your prized pos-
sessions before they pupate.

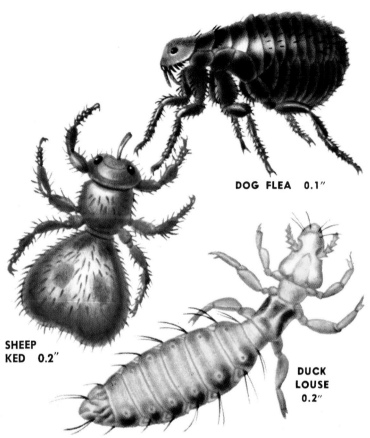

DOG FLEA 0.1"

SHEEP
KED 0.2"

DUCK
LOUSE
0.2"

PESTS OF ANIMALS are many and cause severe losses. Dog fleas spread from dogs to people and may, in some areas, carry plague. They also infest other domestic animals. Control by dusting. Other species are similar. The sheep ked, a species of fly, feeds by sucking blood. The eggs hatch in the body of the female, and the larvae develop to maturity before being deposited. Control is achieved by shearing and dipping the sheep. The squalid duck louse is typical of bird lice (not related to species on page 32) which live on wild and domestic birds.

OTHER COMMON PESTS

The handful of insects that do us considerable harm are reported in this book. Here are some additional examples.

SILVERFISH are primitive, soft-bodied insects which eat starch from bookbindings, wallpaper, and clothing. They are common indoors, especially in warm places.

AMERICAN DOG TICK Not an insect: note its 4 pairs of legs. Common enough and often brought indoors after a walk through fields and woods. Check clothing and body immediately. If attached to skin, remove by touching tick with alcohol. Ticks may transmit serious virus diseases.

BED BUG This flat-bodied household pest, once established, may spread rapidly. May have 3 or 4 generations annually. Female lays white eggs in cracks; eggs hatch in a week or so.

LARDER BEETLE (Dermestes) These small beetles can be serious pests wherever food is stored. The active, hairy larvae feed on all kinds of meat, leather, and other animal products. Four or more generations are produced annually. Widely distributed in the old world and the new.

HOUSE FLY This is the most common and most despised of all the flies. Public health campaigns have not destroyed it. Associated with garbage and filth, flies can reproduce a generation a month when temperatures are favorable. Screening, spraying, swatting, and common-sense sanitation are recommended.

GERMAN COCKROACH or croton bug, introduced from Europe, has become widely established in cities. Like the silverfish it is omnivorous and damages books. Its presence does not necessarily indicate uncleanliness, and it is not a proved carrier of disease like some flies.

SILVERFISH 0.5"

AMERICAN DOG TICK 0.2"

BED BUG 0.3"

LARDER BEETLE 0.3" and larva

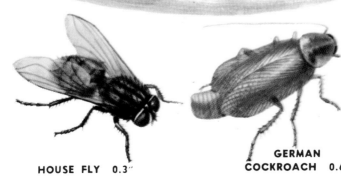

HOUSE FLY 0.3"

GERMAN
COCKROACH 0.6"

FOR MORE INFORMATION

The study of insects requires a balance of what you learn first-hand and what you learn from others. Books and museum exhibits reflect years of research and experience of experts. Collections and field studies must be supplemented by what you read.

MUSEUMS often have systematic, habitat, and local exhibits. Curators are glad to help you identify specimens. Check colleges and universities, as well as large city and state museums. Local inquiries are always best.

BOOKS TO READ The U.S. Dept. of Agriculture and many state departments publish bulletins on insects of economic importance. Write to Supt. of Documents, U.S. Govt. Printing Office, Washington, D.C. 20402, for price list of insect bulletins. Inquire locally for state publications. Some general books are listed below. Try them first before turning to more detailed or technical books.

Arnett, R. H., Jr. and R. L. Jacques. *Simon & Schuster's Guide to Insects*. Simon & Schuster, New York, 1981. An illustrated guide highlighting familiar representative species of the major insect orders.

Borror, D. J. et al. *An Introduction to the Study of Insects*. 4th ed., Holt, Rinehart & Winston, New York, 1976. A technical college text but a good systematic guide. A book for the student who wants to "get his teeth" into the subject.

Borror, D. J. and R. E. White. *A Field Guide to the Insects of America North of Mexico*. The Peterson Field Guide Series, Houghton Mifflin, Boston, 1970. An illustrated guide with natural history information on many species in the major orders.

Milne, L. and A. Milne. *The Audubon Society Field Guide to North American Insects and Spiders*. Alfred A. Knopf, New York, 1980. An illustrated guide to the major orders, with lots of natural history, range information, etc.

Mitchell, Robert T. and Herbert S. Zim. *Butterflies and Moths*. Rev. ed., Golden Press, New York, 1964. A guide to the most common American species, with 423 color illustrations.

Stokes, D. W. *A Guide to Observing Insect Lives*. Little, Brown, Boston & Toronto, 1983. A natural history account of the varied ways in which insects live.

SCIENTIFIC NAMES

Heavy type indicates page where species are illustrated. The genus name is first, then the species. A third name is the subspecies. Occasionally only an order or family name is given. If the genus name is abbreviated, it is the same as the genus name preceding. The abbreviation "spp." indicates that the description applies to more than one species.

17 Diapheromera femorata
18 Bush: Scudderia spp.
   True: Pterophylla
      camellifolia
19 Microcentrum spp.
20 Mole: Neocurtilla
      hexadactyla
   Camel: Ceuthophilus spp.
21 Anabrus simplex
22 Gryllus pennsylvanicus
23 Periplaneta americana
24 Stagmomantis carolina
25 Tenodera aridifolia sinensis
26 American: Schistocerca
      americana
   Carolina: Dissosteira carolina
27 Lubber: Brachystola magna
   Migratory: Melanoplus mexi-
      canus
28 M. femurrubrum
29 Forficula auricularia
30 Reticulitermes spp.
32 Head: Pediculus humanus hu-
      manus
   Short-nosed: Haematopinus eu-
      rysternus
   Crab: Phthirus pubis
   Body: Pediculus humanus corporis
33 Stictocephala bisonia
34 Red-banded: Graphocephala
      coccinea
   Lateral: Cuerna costalis
35 Potato: Empoasca fabae
   3-banded: Erythroneura tricincta
   Rose: Edwardsiana rosae
36 Magicicada septendecim
37 Tibicen spp.
38 Philaenus spumarius
39 Aphidae
40 San Jose: Aspidiotus perniciosus
   Terrapin: Lecanium nigrofasciatum
41 Cottony: Icerya purchasi
   Mealy Bug: Pseudococcus calcoe-
      lariae
   Oystershell: Lepidosaphes ulmi

42 Harlequin: Megantia histronica
   Euschistus: Euschistus spp.
43 Shield: Eurygaster alternata
   Green Stink: Acrosternum
      hilare
44 Anasa tristis
45 Small: Lygaeus kalmii
   Large: Oncopeltus fasciatus
46 Phymata americana
47 Chinch: Blissus leucopterus
   Tarnished: Lygus lineolaris
48 Water Boatman: Corixa spp.
   Backswimmer: Notonecta spp.
49 Water Strider: Gerris spp.
   Giant Water: Lethocerus ameri-
      canus
50 Anax junius
51 Ten-spot: Libellula pulchella
   Blackwing: Calopteryx macu-
      lata
52 Mayfly: Ephemeroptera
   Stonefly: Plecoptera
53 Golden-eye: Chrysopa aculata
   Brown: Hemerobius spp.
54 Corydalus cornutus
55 Myrmeleontidae
56 Panorpha spp.
57 Trichoptera
60 Danaus plexippus
61 Limenitis archippus
62 Banded: L. arthemis
   Red-spotted: L. astyanax
63 Junonia coenia
64 Great Spangled: Speyeria cy-
      bele
   Meadow: Boloria bellona
   Variegated: Euptoieta claudia
   Regal: Speyeria idalia
65 Gulf: Agraulis vanillae
   Silver: Boloria selene
   Regal: Speyeria idalia
66 S. cybele
67 Chalcedon Checkerspot: Occi-
      dryas chalcedona
   Baltimore: Euphydryas phaëton

68 Question Mark: Polygonia inter-rogationis
Comma: P. comma

69 Nymphalis antiopa

70 Amer. Painted Lady: Vanessa vir-giniensis
Red Admiral: V. atalanta

71 V. cardui

72 Eyed Brown: Satyrodes eurydice
Pearly Eye: Enodia portlandia

73 Common Wood: Cercyonis pe-gala
Little Wood: Megisto cymela

74 Gray: Strymon melinus
Purplish: Lycaena helloides
American: L. phlaeas
Bronze: L. hyllus

75 Eastern: Everes comyntas
Marine: Leptotes marina
Spring: Celastrina ladon
Western: Brephidium exilis

76 Pieris rapae

77 Clouded: Colias philodice
Alfalfa: C. eurytheme

78 Spicebush: Papilio troilus
Parnassius: Parnassius smintheus
Giant: Papilio cresphontes

79 Zebra: Eurytides marcellus
Black: Papilio polyxenes
Tiger: P. glaucus

81 Spicebush: P. troilus
Zebra: Eurytides marcellus
Pipevine: Papilio philenor
Black: P. polyxenes
Giant: P. cresphontes
Tiger: P. glaucus

82 Arctic: Carterocephalus palae-mon
Silver-spotted: Epargyreus cla-rus
Southern Cloudy Wing: Thorybes bathyllus

83 Acrea: Estigmene acrea
Isabella: Pyrrharctia isabella

84 Manduca quinquemaculata

85 Hyles lineata

86 Samia cynthia

87 Hyalophora cecropia

88 Callosamia promethea

89 Antheraea polyphemus

90 Automeris io

91 Actias luna

92 Ultronia: Catocala ultronia
Clouded: Euparthenos nubilis

93 Eacles imperialis

94 Earworm: Heliothis zea
Borer: Ostrinia nubilalis

95 Orgyia leucostigma

96 Lymantria dispar

97 Webworm: Hyphantria cunea
Tent: Malacosoma spp.

98 Alsophila pometaria

99 Synanthedon exitiosa

100 Cydia pomonella

101 Thyridopteryx ephemeraeformis

102 Anopheles: Anopheles spp.
Aedes: Aedes spp.

103 Culex spp.

104 Tipula spp.

105 Robber: Asilidae
Deer: Chrysops spp.
March: Bibionidae
Black Horse: Tabanus atratus

106 Bluebottle: Calliphora spp.
Greenbottle: Phaenicia spp.

107 Syrphid: Syrphidae
Tachinid: Tachinidae
Bee Fly: Bombylius major

108 Drosophila melanogaster

109 Six-spotted: Cicindela sexgut-tata
Purple: C. purpurea

110 Macrodactylus subspinosus

111 Popillia japonica

112 Carrion: Silpha americana
Black Carrion: S. ramosa

113 Amer. Burying: Nicrophorus americanus
Hairy Burying: N. tomentosus
Hairy Rove: Creophilus villosus

114 Alaus oculatus

115 Calosoma scrutator

116 Lampyridae

118 Nine-spotted: Coccinella nov-emnotata
Convergent: Hippodamia con-vergens

119 Two-spotted: Adalia bipunc-tata
Fifteen-spotted: Anatis quin-decimpunctata

121 Epilachna varivestis

122 Colo. Potato: Leptinotarsa de-cemlineata
Striped Blister: Epicauta vittata

SCIENTIFIC NAMES (continued)

123 Twelve-spotted: Diabrotica un-
decimpunctata
Striped: Acalymma vittata
125 Common: Crioceris asparagi
Spotted: C. duodecimpunctata
126 Whirligig: Gyrinidae
Dytiscus spp.
127 Hydrophilus triangularis
128 Phyllophaga spp.
129 Cotinus nitida
130 Dung: Phanaeus vindex
Rhinoceros: Xyloryctes satyrus
Tumblebugs: Canthon laevis
131 Ox: Strategus antaneus
Eastern Hercules: Dynastes tityus
132 Horn: Odontotaenius disjunctus
Stag: Pseudolucanus capreolus
133 Darkling: Eleodes spp.
Mealworm: Tenebrio molitor
Tile-horned: Prionus imbricornis
134 Locust: Megacyllene robiniae
Elder: Desmocerus palliatus
Pine Sawyer: Monochamus spp.
Flatheaded: Buprestis rufipes
135 Boll: Anthonomus grandis
Plum: Conotrachelus nenuphar
Nut: Curculio spp.
Billbug: Sphenophorus spp.
136 Tremex columba
137 Megarhyssa atrata
138 Camponotus pennsylvanicus
139 Fire: Solenopsis geminata
Cornfield: Lasius niger
140 Little Black: Monomorium mini-
mum
Pharaoh: M. pharaonis
Argentine: Iridomyrmex humilis
141 Oak Apple: Amphibolips spp.
Elliptical Goldenrod: Gnori-
moshema gallaesolidaginis

141 Goldenrod: Eurosta
solidaginis
Blackberry: Diastrophus spp.
142 Potter: Eumenes fraternus
Mason: Ancistrocerus birene-
maculatus
143 Common Mud: Sceliphron cae-
mentarium
Cuckoo: Chrysis spp.
Blue Mud: Chalybion californi-
cum
144 Velvet Ant: Dasymutilla spp.
Cow-Killer: D. occidentalis
Solitary Wasp: Ammophila au-
reonotata
145 Sphecius speciosus
146 Polistes annularis
147 Bald-faced: Vespula maculata
Yellow Jacket: V. spp.
148 Bumble Bee: Bombus spp.
Sweat Bee: Halictus spp.
149 Leafcutting: Megachile spp.
Honey Bee: Apis mellifera
150 Buffalo Carpet: Anthrenus
scrophulariae
Black Carpet: Attagenus me-
gatoma
Clothes Tinea pellionella
151 Dog Flea: Ctenocephalides
canis
Sheep Ked: Melophagus ovinus
Duck Louse: Lipeurus squalidus
153 Silverfish: Lepisma saccharina
Amer. Dog Tick: Dermacentor
variabilis
Bed Bug: Cimex lectularius
Larder: Dermestes lardarius
House Fly: Musca domestica
Ger. Cockroach: Blatella ger-
manica

158

Asterisks (*) denote pages on which illustrations appear.

MEASURING SCALE (IN MILLIMETERS AND CENTIMETERS)

Acrea moth, *83
Aedes mosquito, *102
Ailanthus silkmoth, *86
Alfalfa butterfly, *77
Ambush bug, *46
American burying beetle, *113
American cockroach, *23
American copper, *74
American dog tick, 152-*153
American grasshopper, *26
American painted lady, *70-71
Angle wings, *68-*69
Angular-winged katydid, *19
Annual cicada, *37
Anopheles mosquito, *102
Ant lions, *55
Antennae, *58
Ants, *138-*140
Aphid lion, 53
Aphids, *39
Aquatic bugs, *48-*49
Arctic skipper, *82
Argentine ant, *140
Asparagus beetles, 124-*125

Backswimmer, *48-49
Bagworm, *101
Bald-faced hornet, 146-*147
Baltimore, *67
Banded purple, *62
Banded woollybear, *83
Bean beetles, 120-*121
Bed bug, 152-*153
Bee fly, *107
Bees, *148-*149
Beetles, *109-*135, *150, 152-*153
Billbug, *135

Black carpet beetle, *150
Black carrion beetle, *112
Black fly, 105
Black swallowtail, *79, 80, *81
Blackberry knot gall, *141
Blackwing damselfly, *51
Blue butterflies, 74-*75
Blue mud dauber, *143
Bluebottle fly, *106
Body louse, *32
Boll weevil, *135
Books, reference, 154
Borers, *94, *134
Bronze copper, *74
Brown lacewing, *53
Brown-tail moth, 96
Buckeye butterfly, *63
Buffalo carpet beetle, *150
Buffalo treehopper, *33
Bugs, *42-*49, 152-*153
Bumble bee, *148
Bush katydid, *18
Butterflies, *58-*82

Cabbage butterfly, *76
Caddisflies, *57
Camel cricket, *20
Cankerworms, *98
Carolina grasshopper, *26
Carolina mantis, *24-25
Carpenter ants, *138
Carrion beetles, *112
Casemaking clothes moth, *150
Caterpillar hunter, *115
Caterpillars, 58-*59, *64-*66, *81
Cave cricket, *20
Cecropia moth, *87
Centipede, *7

Chalcedon checkerspot, *67
Checkerspots, *67
Chinch bug, *11, *47
Cicada killer, *145
Cicadas, *36-*37
Click beetles, *114
Clouded locust underwing moth, *92
Clouded sulphur, *77
Cockroaches, *23, 152-*153
Cocoon, *59
Codling moth, *100
Collecting, 14-16
Colorado potato beetle, 120, *122
Comma, *68
Common mud dauber, 142-*143
Common wood nymph, *73
Convergent ladybird beetle, *118
Copper butterflies, *74
Corn borer, *94
Corn earworm, *94
Cornfield ants, *139
Cottony-cushion scale, *41
Cow-killer wasp, *144
Crab louse, *32
Crane fly, *104
Crickets, *20-*22
Croton bug, 152
Cuckoo wasp, *143
Cucumber beetles, *123, 124
Culex mosquito, 103

Damselflies, 50-*51
Darkling beetles, *133
Darning needles, *50
Deer fly, *105
Diving beetle, *126
Dobsonfly, *54
Dog flea, *151
Doodlebug, *55
Dragonflies, 50-*51

INDEX (continued)

Drone fly, 107
Duck louse, *151
Dung beetle, *130-131

Earwig, *29, 113
Eastern dobsonfly, *54
Eastern Hercules, *131
Eastern tailed blue, *75
Elder borer, *134
Euschistus, *42
Evergreen
    bagworm, *101
Eyed click
    beetle, *114

Fall cankerworm, *98
Field cricket, *22
Fiery searcher, *115
Figeater, 129
Fire ants, *139
Fireflies, *116-*117
Flatheaded borer, *134
Flea, dog, *151
Flies, *11, *104-*108,
    *137, *151-*153
Flower bee, *149
Flower fly, 107
Fritillaries, *64-*65, 66
Froghoppers, 38
Fruit fly, *108

Galls, insect, *141
Garden beetles, 119,
    120-125
German cockroach, 23,
    152-*153
Giant swallowtail, *78,
    80, *81
Giant water bug, *49
Glowworms, 116-117
Golden-eye lacewing,
    *53
Goldenrod galls, *141
Grain weevils, 135
Grasshoppers, *26-*28
Gray hairstreak, *74
Great spangled fritil-
    lary, *64, *66
Green darner, *50
Green June beetle, *129
Greenbottle fly, *106
Gulf fritillary, *65, 66

Gypsy moth, *96

Hairstreaks, *74
Hairy burying beetle,
    *113
Hairy rove beetle, *113
Harlequin bug, *42-43
Harvestfly, 36
Head louse, *32
Hellgrammites, *54
Honey bee, *149
Horn beetle, *132
Hornets, 146-*147
Horntails, *136
Horse fly, black, *105
House fly, *11, *13,
    152-*153
House mosquito, 102-
    *103
Household ants, *140
Household pests, *140,
    *150, 152-*153

Ichneumon, 136, *137
Imperial moth, *93
Insect galls, *141
Insects:
    collecting, 14-16
    control, 9, 124, 152
    development of, *11
    family tree, *10
    parts of, *6, *12-*13
    relatives of, *7
Io moth, *90
Isabella moth, *83

Japanese beetle, *111
June bugs, *128

Katydids, *18-19

Lacewings, *53
Ladybird beetles,
    *118-*119, 120
Ladybug, 118-120
Larder beetle, 152-*153
Larva, *11
Lateral leafhopper, *34
Leafcutting bee, 148-
    *149
Leafhoppers, *34-*35
Lice, *32, *151
Little black ant, *140

Little wood satyr, *73
Locust borer, *134
Locusts, 26
Longhorned borers, 134
Lubber grasshopper,
    *27
Luna moth, *91

Mantises, *24-*25
March fly, *105
Marine blue, *75
Mason wasp, *142
May beetle, *128,
    130
Mayflies, *52
Meadow fritillary, *64
Mealworm beetle, *133
Mealy bug, *41
Melon aphid, *39
Metamorphosis, 11
Mexican bean beetle,
    120-*121
Migratory grasshopper,
    *27
Milkweed bugs, *45
Millipede, *7
Mole cricket, *20
Monarch butterfly, *60
Mormon cricket, *21
Mosquitoes, *102-*103
Moths, 58-59, *83-*101
Mountain butterfly, 80
Mourning cloak, 68,
    *69
Mud wasps, *142-*143
Museums, 154

Northern eyed brown
    butterfly, *72
Nut weevil, *135
Nymphs, *11, *72-*73

Oak apple gall, *141
Ox beetle, *131
Oystershell scale, *41

Painted lady, 70-*71
Paper wasp, *146
Parnassius, *78, 80
Peach tree borer, *99
Pearly-eye butterfly,
    *72-73

INDEX (continued)

Periodical cicada, *36-37
Pests:
  animal, *151, 152-*153
  garden, 124
  household, *140, *150, 152-*153
Pharaoh ant, *140
Pigeon horntail, *136
Pine sawyer, *134
Pipevine swallowtail, 80, *81
Plum curculio, *135
Polyphemus moth, *89
Potato beetles, 120, *122
Potato leafhopper, *35
Potter wasp, *142
Praying mantis, 24-*25
Prionus beetles, *133
Promethea moth, *88
Pupa, *11, *59
Purple tiger beetle, *109
Purples, *62
Purplish copper, *74

Question mark, *68

Range maps, use of, 3
Red admiral, *70
Red-banded leafhopper, *34
Red-legged grasshopper, *28
Red-spotted purple, *62
Regal fritillary, *64-*65
Regal moth, 93
Rhinoceros beetle, *130
Robber fly, *105
Rose chafer, *110, 130
Rose leafhopper, *35
Roundheaded borers, *133
Rove beetles, 113

San Jose scale, *40
Satyrs, *72-*73
Sawflies, 136
Scale insects, *40-*41

Scarab beetles, 110, *111, 120, *128, *130-*131, 132
Scientific names, 155-157
Scorpionflies, *56
Sheep ked, *151
Shield bugs, 42-*43
Short-nosed cattle louse, *32
Silk moth, *86
Silver-bordered fritillary, *65
Silverfish, *11, 152-*153
Silver-spotted skipper, *82
Six-spotted tiger beetle, *109
Skipper butterflies, *82
Solitary wasps, *144, *145
Southern cloudy wing skipper, *82
Sowbug, 7
Sphinx moths, *84-*85
Spicebush moth, 88
Spicebush swallowtail, *78, 80, *81
Spiders, *7
Spittlebug, *38
Spotted asparagus beetle, 124-*125
Spring azure, *75
Squash bugs, *44
Stag beetles, *132
Stink bugs, 42-*43
Stoneflies, *52
Striped blister beetle, 120, *122
Striped cucumber beetle, *123, 124
Sulphurs, *77
Swallowtails, *78-*81
Sweat bee, *148
Syrphid fly, *107

Tachinid fly, *44, *107
Tarnished plant bug, *47
Ten-spot dragonfly, *51
Tent caterpillar, *97
Termites, *30-*31
Terrapin scale, *40

Thistle butterfly, 71
Three-banded leafhopper, *35
Ticks, 152-*153
Tiger beetles, *109
Tiger swallowtail, *79, 80, *81
Tile-horned prionus, *133
Tobacco worm, 84
Tomato hornworm, *84
Treehoppers, *33
Tumblebug, *130-131
Tussock moth, *95, 96
Twelve-spotted cucumber beetle, *123, 124

Ultronia underwing moth, *92
Underwing moths, *92

Variegated fritillary, *64
Velvet ant, *144
Viceroy butterfly, *61
Violet-tip, 68

Walkingsticks, *17
Wasps, *142-*147
Water beetles, *126-*127
Water-boatmen, *48-49
Water bugs, *48-*49
Water scavenger, *127
Water striders, *49
Water tigers, *126-127
Webworm, fall, *97
Weevils, *135
Western blues, *75
Whirligig beetles, *126-*127
White ants, 30
White-faced hornet, 146-*147
Wireworms, *114
Woollybear, *83

Yellow jackets, 146-*147

Zebra swallowtail, *79, 80, *81